DOING QUALITATIVE
RESEARCH
FOR BEGINNERS

DOING QUALITATIVE
RESEARCH
FOR BEGINNERS
FROM THEORY TO PRACTICE

ISMAIL SHEIKH AHMAD (PH.D.)

PARTRIDGE

To order additional copies of this book, contact
Toll Free 800 101 2657 (Singapore)
Toll Free 1 800 81 7340 (Malaysia)
orders.singapore@partridgepublishing.com

www.partridgepublishing.com/singapore

Contents

Author's Note

The strength of this book lies in the simplicity of sharing the concepts and practices in qualitative research methods. It epitomises the basic know-how in grasping the qualitative research world.

Qualitative research methods have gained popularity inside and outside the academic world. Researchers have shown growing interest in understanding an issue through qualitative, and not just quantitative, lenses. Researchers are well aware of the challenges in making sense of the qualitative paradigm. In one sense, the qualitative concepts are rather different than the quantitative ones, and the data interpretations in generating the themes are rather recursive in the quest of arriving at the findings.

Qualitative Research for Beginners is fundamental enough to those researchers who are new to qualitative research methods. In the author's humble opinion, this book will be useful in guiding the researchers to understand and appreciate the basic nature in conducting qualitative research. Readers will find the book full of simple examples and illustrations in guiding them to understand the concepts and know-how in data gathering, analysing, and reporting qualitative findings meaningfully. Qualitative research connotes contextually rich or "thick" data. In making sense of such information, the author provides adequate samples and mechanisms to reduce the rich information to meaningful findings. The author's practical applied approach and straightforward writing style make this book easy to understand, thus helping researchers with their research projects.

The book is rather unique in several ways that are important to the beginners and presented in an applied manner. It provides

- an overview of the underlying issues in differentiating qualitative and quantitative research;
- basic approaches and process flows in conducting qualitative research;
- an extensive discussion on steps in conducting a doable qualitative research project; and
- a basic tool in reporting the qualitative findings.

Preface and Acknowledgements

The main objective of *Qualitative Research for Beginners* is to provide a simple guide to novice researchers in the world of qualitative research by understanding the what, or fundamental concepts of qualitative paradigm, as well as the basic tools, or how, in preparing qualitative research proposal, data gathering, data analyses, and data reporting techniques. The inspiration to prepare the content of this qualitative book comes from numerous related scholarly works and applied fields. It draws on many related research studies, previous experiences in conducting qualitative courses, and training of qualitative researchers in private and government agencies in Malaysia.

A number of people have helped me in the production of this book as well as referring me to a number of major players in the field of known qualitative authors, such as John W. Creswell; A. Michael Huberman; and Matthew B. Miles. Thanks to all of my former postgraduate qualitative research students and PhD supervisees for their useful discussions and insights in inspiring me to complete the writing journey. I would like to thank my main supervisor, Emeritus Professor Colin Harrison (Literacy Studies in Education, the University of Nottingham, England), who introduced me to the world of qualitative research back in the 1990s.

Introduction

Introducing new researchers with little background in the concepts and theories of qualitative research, as well as guiding them in completing qualitative research projects, is full of challenges. The purpose of this book is to help the new researchers, undergraduate and postgraduate students in particular, and other educational practitioners with little or no background in qualitative research to grasp the basic underpinnings of qualitative research paradigms and the know-how of completing a basic qualitative research project.

Focussing on the fundamental needs of new researchers in understanding qualitative paradigm, I decided to present the content of the book in a more practical way, yet supported by scholarly references. Thus, the book advances a process-oriented framework in designing a qualitative research for beginners who seek assistance in preparing for a research project or a scholarly dissertation or thesis.

In understanding the "how", I present examples of successful templates from the beginning of a proposal to a number of systematic steps in data analysis. Furthermore, explanations are given to each template, which avoids presenting it in a theoretical manner but focusses on how to conduct a qualitative study from beginning to end. In this way, a new qualitative researcher can learn how to generate a research problem, ask central and research questions, and collect and analyse the data.

Since there are different types of qualitative data, it made sense to give due attention to the interview process, which is the most common method of data collection in qualitative research. There is no specific qualitative software used in guiding the researchers. The intention is to expose them to the fundamental methodological approach in conducting the study, and due attention is given to qualitative data analysis.

The underlying approach and design of this book is research-based as well as utilising the author's experiences in teaching qualitative research content at the International Islamic University Malaysia (IIUM) for more than a decade and conducting real-world qualitative research training in the government and private agencies in Malaysia. The book simplifies the basic differences between the qualitative and quantitative perspectives. This fundamental differences are crucial in mapping the minds of the new researchers from the very beginning of the course because sometimes prior knowledge in quantitative perspectives can lead to fundamental conflicts with new qualitative information. This is notable when it touches certain fundamental differences on data generalisation and the concept of reliability and validity of quantitative perspectives against its equivalent, such as credibility and trustworthiness.

Chapter 1attempts to trace the basic and fundamental attributional differences between qualitative and quantitative perspectives. Basic fundamental questions – for example, why certain qualitative research is chosen for a particular research project, as shown through a bird's eye view of the process flow in qualitative research – are explained. The author's experiences in teaching PhD and DBA courses (EDF 7810, advanced qualitative research methods, and MGT 7312, qualitative and case research methodologies, respectively), supervising postgraduate qualitative research theses, as well as conducting qualitative studies for the private and governmental agencies in Malaysia have triggered the importance of the researchers to understand the fundamental differences of five basic approaches to qualitative research: ethnography, grounded theory, phenomenology, case study, and narrative.

The process flow in doing qualitative research is explained in chapter 2. The journey begins with the fundamental concepts on central phenomenon, research problem, the central question, and research questions. This chapter clarifies the importance of understanding the interconnectedness between the central question and research questions in light of the research problem. This is the most fundamental phase, where the thinking of the researchers needs to be objectively stated. In fact, the author's experienced a lot of challenges in delivering the content of this phase. It is more than just leading the thinking of the researchers to a certain doable research topic. The researchers must reflect whether the questions are clear and representative enough of the issue and problem raised in the background of the study. This is where the reiterative nature in understanding the gist of the research problem and preparing the questions need to be clearly understood. It is not a simple one-way flow they might have presumed at the beginning of the course. We instead focus on a type of qualitative research data as a fundamental tool in data gathering technique: the interview. A simple technique, known as FABB (facts, attitudes, beliefs, and behaviours), guides the formation of the research questions as well as the interview questions.

The fundamental and systematic flow in generating qualitative data is further explained in chapter 3. This is where the stages in piloting, collecting real data, analysing and categorising the data, and theme generating are explained. The importance of understanding the know-how in organising and interpreting the data is crucial in the quest of producing credible data interpretation-cum-findings. Albeit being deductive in approach due to the predetermined organising, categorising, analysing, and theme-generating templates, the author cannot escape from the fact that the researchers must be taught the fundamentals of qualitative data analyses in generating the proper main ideas and themes from the emic (relating to an approach of the study or description of a particular language or culture in terms of its internal elements and their functioning rather than in terms of any existing external scheme) perspective. The importance of inter-rater reliability in qualitative research is further elaborated. The generated themes should be independently coded by raters and the codings compared for agreements to ensure the credibility of the themes. Performing inter-rater reliability would inform the researchers on a number of issues, such as the quality of the generated themes and rogue coders.

Reporting or presenting qualitative data is a challenge to the new qualitative researchers. In some cases, it is seen as confusing and time consuming. In many circumstances, reporting qualitative findings is more often in the form of the generated themes. Thus, a pragmatic approach, such as using a formula called describe-compare-relate (DCR), guides the writing process. Although this is deductive in approach, it is seen as a fundamental step in reporting the findings. The author suggests a simple qualitative writing-up checklist as well as a systematic flow in forwarding a new macro concept or model as a research contribution. The new concept or model should be seen as a potential knowledge in theory building or knowledge expansion.

Chapter 1

Underlying Issues and Fundamental Knowledge in Understanding Qualitative Research

Not everything that can be counted counts, and not everything that counts can be counted.
—Sociologist William Bruce Cameron

1.1 Differentiating between Qualitative and Quantitative Perspectives

Throughout more than a decade of teaching qualitative research in a higher learning institution, the author has seen postgraduate students and novice researchers struggle to understand the rudiments of the qualitative research paradigm and its practical ramifications. Understanding the core concepts that demarcate quantitative from qualitative modalities and their respective unique applications, as well as their distinct styles of data analyses and reportage, are absolutely crucial in order to avoid the tedium and repetitiousness of trial and error, one-size-fits-all researching, which rarely ends up finding anything at all.

The author has encountered many novice researchers being familiar with the quantitative paradigm while facing difficulties in shifting and adjusting their "quantified" mind to one especially identifying the underlying themes and later explaining the phenomenon. Through experience, the author has become acquainted with postgraduate students possessing a naive view of qualitative research being a second-class research perspective without understanding the concept of evidence in the qualitative paradigm, which necessitates a whole new way of thinking in understanding the notion of evidence in research.

Sandeloswki (2004) observed the same phenomenon. Qualitative research is thick with words rather than numbers alone, which novice researchers should be aware of. Table 1 summarises the fundamental attributes and differences between the qualitative and quantitative research perspectives:

Table 1.1 Fundamental Differences between Qualitative and Quantitative Research

Fundamental Characteristics	Quantitative Research	Qualitative Research
Scope of study	Narrow and specific inquiry or hypothesis	Generalized and broadly observed phenomenon
Data category	Data-orientated towards quantification and numeric	Narration based reports leading towards in depth comprehension of the issue
Data collection techniques	Pre formulated and rigidly structured as seen in questionnaires	Adaptive inquiry tools such as in-depth interviews, group discussions, and documents

Interpretation paradigm	Descriptive and inferential statistical-based perspectives	Discovering underlying concepts or themes to be weaved into comprehensible concepts/models
Primary strength	Large sampling lead towards statistical validity that is reflective of the population	Saturated and in-depth narration describing the notions of the informants
Main weakness	The possibility of being superficial in generalizing the thoughts of the respondents to the population	Too specific to the case studied that it is not generalizable to the population

Table 1.1 illustrates the major differences of the two research perspectives through the lenses of six major attributes:

- scope of study;
- data category;
- data-collection technique;
- interpretation paradigm;
- primary strength; and
- main weakness.

The nature of qualitative research is rather "thick" in describing the deeper understanding of a phenomenon through the term *findings*, as opposed to *results*; the former is associated with qualitative as represented by themes or categories, and the latter is a known term in quantitative methodology and represented by numerical data. In many cases, qualitative data involves case research study and is purposive in its sampling technique of targeted informants or respondents. The selected informants are thought to be able to share rich information pertaining to a selected issue or issues to be investigated. The rich data would come from various data collecting techniques seen as important and feasible in explaining the targeted phenomenon, and in return would answer the notion of credibility and trustworthiness of the research findings.

1.2 Decision Matters: Why Embark on a Qualitative Research Project?

The decision to conduct a qualitative research, bearing in mind that methodologically neither the qualitative nor the quantitative method is intrinsically better or superior, depends on how the research problem is being posed. It requires fundamental knowledge, especially upon the notion of what works in finding answers to the what, how, and why questions of a selected phenomenon.

A researcher must justify and decide as to why a qualitative perspective is needed in light of the issue and the research questions. As an example, a case study may be seen as an appropriate research strategy in providing the best qualitative information in explaining the issue. Yin (1994, 9) suggests that a case study's appropriate how or why questions arise during a contemporary set of events over which the investigator has little or no control.

In one of the author's previous qualitative studies, the process of understanding how and why a group of students responded to a number of comprehension questions is viewed as a challenging and time-consuming effort. Thus, for the study, the students were immediately interviewed after completing a comprehension test. The author believed the interview was the best method in understanding the reasoning processes used by the students in answering the comprehension questions, with the assumption that the how and why information was still fresh in the informants' minds. All of the interviews were cautiously done, thus avoiding the likelihood of assisting the informants on their reasoning processes and maintaining the need to gather quality information.

In light of the above situation, basic training in handling a fruitful interview is essential. Adaptable and flexible interviewing skills would have to be understood to ensure quality information is received from the informants. The technique employed for the author's above case is reflective of the approach described by Robson (1993), Cohen, Manion & Morrison (2011), and Yin (2014) and is deemed as anticipative of any nonverbal cues that may provide information on the informants' thoughts and perceptions relatable to each individual's personality. Essentially, an interview session must allow the collection of essential information in a friendly and non-intimidating atmosphere (Robson 1993).

In this context, the author has observed novice researchers "putting the cart before the horse" in their planning of the research method. It is not the choice of whether to conduct the research quantitatively or qualitatively but rather the perspective of the researchers in viewing the selected issue or phenomenon and later selecting the best data-collecting method for each research question. In some cases, a mixed-method research design would seem appropriate to understand the phenomenon. If the quantified survey data provides answers to the "what" aspect or the extent of the phenomenon, then the qualitative aspect provides deeper understanding of the intricate and deeper questions of how and why a group of teenagers is involved in drug abuse, their experiences, and the challenges they faced. Clearly, the background of the issue(s), later reflected in a number of research questions and the kind of data needed to provide information to best explain the issue(s), would certainly colour the research methodology.

In many cases the author would recommend researchers to first clear the air and identify whether the phenomenon is seen as rather new or less known in the literature review. If the related theories of the phenomenon are lacking – or, in other words, less is known of the phenomenon – researchers would need to do an initial literature review about the selected phenomenon, and as more inputs are gathered from the collected qualitative data, the researchers need to update the literature relevant to the inputs. More often than not, it is observed that the researchers changed or adjusted the research questions due to new findings in the literature that have shaped the perspectives of the researchers in viewing the phenomenon. Significantly, researchers need to immerse themselves as much as possible by collecting preliminary information on the informants' experiences, beliefs, behaviours, and attitudes towards the phenomenon through field observations such as interviews and engaging themselves with the informants in the field.

This dual concurrent preliminary data collecting activities of the contextualized reality of the phenomenon and the corresponding new development in the literature would allow better perspectives in shaping the research questions. Thus, the iterative nature of the qualitative research process would allow more meaningful findings in explaining the phenomenon under study (see figure 1.1)

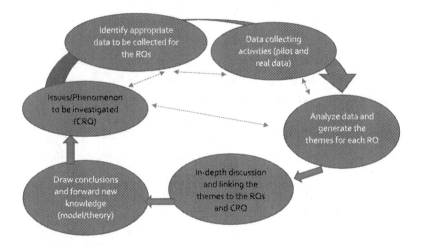

Figure 1.1 The Process Flow of Qualitative Research

Figure 1.1 simplifies the basic cyclic nature in conducting a qualitative research in an academic setting. Basically, the researchers need to identify and understand the topic to be studied and its underlying issues and problems. Once a draft of the phenomenon is converted into a simplified central research question (CRQ), the relevant research questions (RQs), and the types of data to be collected for each RQ, the researchers may pilot them in the field. More often than not, there will be modifications to the issues, CRQ, RQs, and the data-collecting tools based on the inputs from the piloting activities. In some cases, as shown by the thin arrows, there would be several piloting activities in assuring the robustness of the data-collecting instrument, such as the interview questions, participant-observation procedures, and the number of informants or respondents to be sampled. In fact, there could be several drafts before a decision is made as to the best research design for the phenomenon to be studied.

At the crux of the process flow in table 1.2 is the notion of finding the best research design or good fit of each RQ with the type of data that can provide the richest possible source of information in explaining the phenomenon as stated by the RQs. This would entail, for example, a purposive or snowball sampling technique that would influence the best settings possible, such as events and related activities in the quest of assuring the best and richest data possible in explaining the phenomenon.

Qualitative research involves looking in-depth at non-numerical data thus requiring the researchers to reflect critically in choosing a proper design. This entails understanding the basic fundamental qualitative research design. McCaslin and Scott (2003) suggest the basic five-question method in framing the intended qualitative inquiry, as explained in table 1.2.1:

Table 1.2.1 Five Questions to Select the "Colour" to Paint a Qualitative Design

Questions to Ask to Discover the Preferred Approach	Associated Tradition
If I could discover the meaning of one person's lived experience, I would ask _____ (individual) about _____.	Biography
If I could discover the shared lived experiences of one quality or phenomenon in others, I would want to know about _____.	Phenomenology

If I could experience a different culture by living/ observing it, I would choose to experience _____.	Ethnography
If I could discover what actually occurred and was experienced in a single lived event, that event would be _____.	Case Study
If I could discover a theory for a single phenomenon of living as shared by others, I would choose to discover the theory of _____.	Grounded Theory

Source: Mark L. McCaslin and Karen Wilson Scott (2003)

Table 1.2.1 serves as a guide in building the skills to reflect upon the key fundamental questions out of the research problems aimed for the research and the corresponding qualitative research traditions. In short, a research question could be seen from any of the five traditions as long as it is justified as the best suitable perspective in light of the issues and background of the research problems. Thus, an issue can be investigated using a combination of the five traditions.

Alternatively, the main differences between qualitative and quantitative research tools are provided by Ledgerwood and White (2006) in the following table.

Table 1.2.2 The Differences between Qualitative and Quantitative Research Tools

Method Matrix	Qualitative Research	Quantitative Research
Objective	To gain in-depth understanding of consumers' attitudes and behaviours	To measure the degree and extent of the attitudes

Confidence level	Explorative, anecdotal	Conclusive, with a specified degree of certainty
Techniques	Unstructured or semi-structured	Structured
Tools	Focus groups, in-depth interviews, mystery shoppers	Simple and complex surveys, database analysis (cross tabulation)
Participants	Small and homogeneous groups	Samples with a statistical representation of the population
Results	Words and descriptions	Codified results, compiled as statistics
Training and preparation	Understanding objectives of the study	Consistency and precision of questions used computer analysis
Strengths	In-depth exploration of questions. Better understanding of underlying behaviours. Usually can implement with staff	Conclusive; its results can be inferred to the rest of the population. Better for costly investment because it measures degree and frequency of behaviours
Weaknesses	Subjective; bias can be introduced in the execution and analysis of results not conclusive; research cannot be inferred to the population	Bias on the form and the questionnaire can be costly and time consuming. Usually implemented by outside marketing research firms

Table 1.2.2 summarises the fundamental methodological differences between qualitative and quantitative research viewed from the objective, confidence level, techniques, tools, participants, results, training and preparation, strengths, and weaknesses. In the case of results, quantitative research expresses its results in terms of statistical inputs rather than thick descriptions of findings in qualitative dimension. In terms of sampling the respondents or participants, quantitative research seeks statistical representation as

opposed to specified targeted small numbers of informants through non-probability purposive or snowball sampling techniques. In fact, in qualitative research, the researchers play a key role in gathering and interpreting the data from the informants. This notion is known as "researcher as research instrument" and if not addressed properly, it can be a threat to the credibility and trustworthiness of the research itself, such as researcher biases in preparing and defending the quality and integrity of the instrument and thus risking the quality of the research project. Biases can be in the form of the state of mind of the researcher, data-collecting skills and proper preparation, as well as the degree of the researcher's affinity with the targeted group under study (Denzin and Lincoln 2000, 368; Marshall and Rossman 1995, 59–65).

1.3 Basic Approaches to Qualitative Research

Qualitative researchers need to understand the underlying approaches to qualitative research and how they are related to the targeted research topic or issue. In general, there are five known approaches to qualitative research as follows:

Ethnography

It is a qualitative approach studying the cultural elements of participants of a selected group in their natural settings. The study encompasses more than the traditional meaning of a culture of an ethnic group but has grown to studying the cultural patterns and perspectives of an organisation over time in search of the underlying essence of shared concepts, beliefs, attitudes, behaviours or practices, and language. Due to the interconnectedness of the elements of the term *culture*, an ethnographer must spend time with the participants through fieldwork, in some cases taking years to make sense of the targeted culture. Broadly speaking, the ethnographer would investigate the cultural patterns of the targeted group by looking into the cultural beliefs, know-how, and orientation through participant observation and interview. Thus, the ethnographer must be immersed in the daily routines of the targeted culture or selected key informants and record the experiences by describing, analysing, and interpreting the experiences.

Grounded Theory

Generating a new theory by interpreting qualitative data, as opposed to testing new theory, is the ultimate aim of grounded theory (Glaser and Strauss 1967; Strauss and Corbin 1994). It requires a set of important steps, which is iterative in nature, or theoretical methods unique to grounded theory as summarised by Birks and Mills (2011, 9–10) as consisting of

(1) initial coding and categorization of data;
(2) concurrent data generation or collection and analysis;
(3) writing memos; theoretical sampling; constant comparative analysis using inductive and abductive logic;
(4) theoretical sensitivity;
(5) intermediate coding;
(6) selecting a core category;
(7) theoretical saturation; and
(8) theoretical integration.

Data from these initial encounters is coded before more data is collected or generated. This concept differentiates grounded theory from other types of research design that required the researcher to initially collect and subsequently analyse the data, or to construct a theoretical proposition and then collect data to test their hypothesis.

An example of a grounded theory is seen through the implementation of the process approach. Through the approach, grounded theorists would explore the underlying processes or action and interactions of the targeted people pertaining to a research topic, and in so doing, themes or categories are generated in the form of *in vivo* codes or the original verbatim from the participants rather than from the interpretation of the researchers. The coding would allow a compounding accumulation of information, developing categories founded upon the previously discovered themes in the process. This is a process seen similar to the building of a pyramid, which would ultimately peak at answering the Central Research Question (CRQ) and an in-depth understanding of the phenomenon.

Phenomenology

A phenomenological paradigm is a method of inquiry associated with German philosophers Edmund Husserl and Martin Heidegger. It attempts to capture the subjective experiences and interpretations as perceived by the participants or group of people in an unbiased manner. How they view and understand the world from their perspectives would be the focal point of the phenomenologists. Thus, the main goal of phenomenology is to understand the "life world" as viewed and experienced by the participants. It requires researchers to free themselves from any preconceptions and interferences. This method allows them to understand the informants' subjective world in their own terms, making them visible and true to the informants' views and experiences. Phenomenology is also seen as one of the most widely used approaches in qualitative methodology. However, it is essential to note that researching through the phenomenological perspective would require researchers to avoid hypothesis testing or the utilisation of theoretically guided Research Questions (RQs).

Case Study

A case study could be technically defined as an empirical investigation of a contemporary phenomenon done in depth and within its real-life context in the absence of a clear boundary between the phenomenon and context. It will allow researchers to place technical intricacies of having multiple variables of interest besides the data point, be receptive towards multiple sources of evidence that need to be converged and triangulated, as well as build up the study by benefiting from previously established theoretical propositions for data collection and analysis. It should be noted that all the data collection should be done systematically with standardized procedures in place.

A researcher would need to acquire an understanding of other research methods to gain exposure towards other previously done case studies or experiments that may be exploratory, descriptive, and explanatory in behaviour. This will allow an informed decision to employ the most advantageous research approach to be implemented in the case study. It is important that the researcher aligns the previous studies in accordance to the RQs; the control a researcher has over actual behavioural events; and the relevance of the current research focus with the historical settings of the previous studies.

Thus, understanding the type of RQs raised by the researchers is crucial, and if the how and why questions are raised, the favourable research method would fit case studies, histories, or experiments. A research question may fit a number of methods, and a careful distinction must be made as to the appropriate method or combination of methods in light of the issues and corresponding research questions.

Creswell (2012, 465) considers a case study as a type of ethnography but with the researchers' "focus on a program, event, or activity involving individuals rather than a group per se".

In comparison, an ethnographer may generalise shared patterns of the targeted group over time, and a case study researcher may look at a micro level or the deeper parts of the phenomenon of the group.

Of further note, a case study may also be

(1) a series of steps that constitutes a sequence of events, such as a curriculum development process;

(2) an exceptional or unusual event occurring as a unique phenomenon in a community, such as the underlying motivation amongst avid readers in school; and

(3) an effort to collect multiple forms of data for an in-depth understanding of a case, such as collecting pictures, historical documents, or letters to understand a country's independence struggle.

Narrative Research

The term itself connotes telling an in-depth specific story pertaining to individuals or events. An example would be a study about individual experiences being explored and discussed in a literary manner such as a researcher opting to report on the experiences and meaning of an international student studying in a university in Malaysia by collecting what he or she attributes to the story using a combination of tools, such as interviews, observations, and other related documents. The researcher must create a close rapport and communication with the informant in the quest to capture the depth of the experiences, following a chronology of events that may include information on facts, beliefs, attitudes, and behaviours or processes. Generally, this approach is time consuming, so for student researchers, only a few participants should be the case subjects.

Basically, there are four possible types of narrative research:

- An oral history provides deep reflections of certain incidences or events analyzing relevant aspects, such as the pros and cons, effects and problems.
- Auto-ethnography is done through self-reporting by the informants, collected using mediums such as a journal, log, or digital recording.
- A life history is recorded through the collection of records or historical documents of a person.
- A biography captures the experiences of an individual.

To sum, qualitative research is a form of social inquiry on how the informants interpret and make sense of their life experiences and the world they live in. It goes deeper and is far richer than numbers. Due to this delicateness in making sense of the informants' world, this chapter shows a bird's eye view on the fundamental knowledge in qualitative research. It focuses on basic differences between qualitative and quantitative perspectives as well as some basic approaches in qualitative paradigm.

Chapter 2

Fundamental Steps in Conducting Qualitative Research and Related Issues

There is a hidden treasure inside every problem. It's your job to find it.

—Author Unknown

Qualitative methods seek to answer questions pertaining to the how, what, or why of a phenomenon as experienced by the informants. The following steps are provided to shed light on the collecting research data method of semi-structured interviews, which is one the most common data-collection methods.

2.1 Step 1: Identifying a Research Problem

The first step in identifying a research problem requires the researcher to reflect on the phenomenon to be studied. A problem could be based on personal experiences, experiences shared by others or previous studies highlighting the need to investigate further the results or findings from the qualitative perspective. In a way, if little is known of a phenomenon, for example its underlying characteristics, even after a rigorous literature search or review of the published or unpublished databases was done, then it is a good start for an exploration on the underlying characteristics of a phenomenon. Significantly, if the intent is to understand and probe deeper the perspectives of the informants and explore the related meaning given to the phenomenon, then qualitative design is seen as appropriate.

A researcher may begin reflecting on a phenomenon of interest by finding the answers to several basic questions, such as:

- What is the issue to be addressed? That would essentially help the researcher to look into the phenomenon more objectively.
- What are the situational catalysts that would require the study to be done? That would assist the researcher to identify the occurrence of the phenomenon in a real-life scenario either on individuals or society.
- What is the underlying concern to be addressed through the study? That would require the researcher to identify the impact of the phenomenon and its investigation.
- What solutions could the study offer? That would outline the possible findings, implications, and significance of the study.

Hence, as an example, in an issue involving the growing numbers of adolescent girls participating in cigarette smoking activities in an urban school, the reflection could be observed as follows.

- The issue to be addressed is the growing number of adolescent girls participating in cigarette smoking.
- The situational catalyst would be statistical data that indicates the growing number of smokers amongst adolescent girls.
- If the phenomenon is not investigated, it may reflect or influence society's overall health outlook, or it may affect the social and cultural harmony as well as being perceived as a behaviour that may be against certain religious tenets.
- The study may help develop an understanding of why adolescent girls were involved in the activity, thus allowing for a list of mitigating and controlling actions to be done to curb the situation.

Thus, upon reflection, the researcher would have gained a strong foundation of research problem, which in turn would be a guiding principle of all the actions taken in the course of the research.

Remember, a research problem should not be confused with a research topic. Throughout the authors' involvement with budding qualitative researchers, they often perceive that the two – the research problem and the research topic – are interchangeably used, but this is not the case. A research topic is the general subject matter addressed in a study. Using the above scenario, the research *topic* may be adolescent girls' health, but the research *problem* is a more specified issue being addressed by the study. In this case it is the smoking habits of the adolescent girls.

2.2 Step 2: Purpose Statement and Research Questions

Once the fundamental basis of the need to conduct qualitative research is justified, a purpose statement, written as an open-ended statement capturing information of the phenomenon, is required. A good purpose statement should state the major focus of the research study, while a good qualitative purpose statement should include the intent of the study, a central phenomenon to be investigated, the participants or informants involved, and the research site.

For example, relevant to the case above, the purpose statement could be written as, "The purpose of this study is to explore teachers' views on smoking amongst female students in three selected secondary schools in Kuala Lumpur".

Writing good qualitative research question requires proper guidelines. Basically, a researcher would like to capture rich information from the participants or informants (termed *emic,* or data from participants' words), as well as data from previous research studies or literature (or *etic*, outside the perspective of the observer).

Let us say that a selected topic has little theoretical and conceptual content attached to it, which requires the researcher to focus on the generated themes or categories of ideas from the participants. A researcher would want to capture as much information as possible throughout the investigation, and a "backbone" question – also known as a central research question (CRQ) – is needed to steer the course of the research question. A reasonable CRQ requires key information such as the key phenomenon to be investigated, the targeted research site, and participants or informants. Once a CRQ is established, it will act as a canopy or an umbrella from which a number of research questions (RQs) will emanate, providing specific questions to be studied in light of the research problem. In a nutshell, the research questions should address a number of questions that, once executed, would provide rich data for the CRQ.

Figure 2.1 (see below) illustrates the connection between the CRQ and RQs. The good fit between the CRQ and RQs reflects the idea that the RQs are clearly written and should be able to generate the necessary information or data in explaining the CRQ, which in turn should be able to explain the issue out of the observed phenomenon as outlined in the research problem. In a nutshell, the concisely written and adequate RQs act as the middle agent in representing the research problems. The RQs must be adequate, credible, and reasonable enough to generate valid accounts of the phenomenon. Additionally, the RQs should capture the essence of the phenomenon as represented in the CRQ.

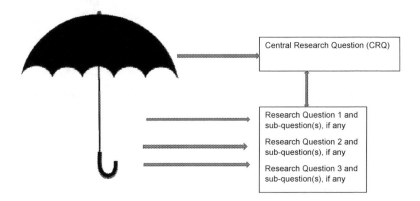

Figure 2.1 The Interconnectedness between the CRQ and RQs.

2.3 Step 3: Generating Interview Questions

The process of generating the interview questions is recursive in nature. Each research question must be represented by adequate interview questions. More often than not, novice researchers are clueless as to how many interview questions would be enough for each research question. For example, in light of conducting research using semi-structured interview questions, they should be able to trigger the conversation and capture the information pertaining to the phenomenon. It is important to remember that the semi-structured interview questions are the main guiding questions, and subsequent probing questions would depend on the oral responses of the informants and the probing skills of the researchers in conducting the interview.

As a rule of thumb, when the researcher has reached a saturation point for an interview question, whereby no more information can be gathered or the informant has no more information to be shared, the researcher should proceed to the next question. The flow of asking the interview questions may not be as orderly as desired by the researcher.

The researcher must know and be aware as to what kind of information is shared and the adequacy of the information, and he or she should adjust the ordering of the interview questions based on the context and flow of the interview. Bear in mind that an interview is a conversation with a purpose, and it should be in a natural yet relaxed setting. Conducting an interview in a stressful setting may make the informant uneasy, thus making it more difficult to elicit information.

There is no precise rule as to the number of interview questions for each of the research questions. Basically, it is generally between three and five questions, and the number must be judged adequate to generate the information needed to explain the phenomenon.

Interview questions can be categorised into four basic dimensions; **f**acts, **a**ttitudes, **b**eliefs, and **b**ehaviours (FABB). FABB questions serve as a guide in generating the interview questions. In many cases the Interview Questions (IQs) or even the RQs were modified after piloting the interview questions. These inevitable changes in constructing valuable qualitative work is part and parcel of the recursive nature of qualitative research and is very much related to the credibility and trustworthiness of the data. It is crucial at this juncture to understand the notion of behaviours. It should also be thought of as processes thus related to the "how" dimension of the phenomenon.

The following are examples of the FABB types of IQs.

Table 2.1 Types of FABB and Corresponding Interview Questions

Types of Question	Examples of Interview Questions
Facts	• How many cigarettes do you smoke a day? • Are you involved in the activity? How and Why?
Attitudes	• How do you handle mistakes? • How do you handle negative comments by your superior? • When faced with a difficult task, how do you react to it?
Beliefs	• How do you define justice in your organization? • Is trustworthiness importance in your organization? Why?
Behaviours	• How do you handle stress? • What obstacles did you face, and how did you overcome them? • How did you find the tasks assigned to you? • How do you manage your time?

Table 2.2 (below) shows an example of the interconnectedness-cum-good fit amongst the CRQ, RQs, and IQs. The IQs have yet to be piloted, and changes may occur to some of the RQs, IQs, or even

the CRQ. In some cases, the researchers may change his or her mind on the topic after the piloting activities due to feedback received from the field. Again, adjusting and refining the CRQ, RQs, and IQs are important activities that would add rigour to the data.

Table 2.2 Central Research Question, Research Questions, and Interview Questions

Central Research Question (CRQ)	Research Questions/ Subquestions (RQs/ SQs)	Interview Questions (IQs)
What does smoking cigarettes means to addicted female smokers in three selected secondary schools in Kuala Lumpur?	How do the addicted female students define smoking?	• How long have you been smoking cigarettes? • Do you remember why you started smoking? • How often do you smoke? Any specific brand? Why? • How do you feel about your addiction/smoking habit? • How do you feel if you have not had a cigarette for a period of time? Why? • What is smoking to you, then?

	1. What are contributing factors leading to the addictive smoking activities? 1.1 What kind of settings lead to the smoking activities?	• What are the reasons that have triggered you to smoke and later become addicted to it? • Are you smoking alone or socially? Why? • What sort of circumstances trigger you to smoke? • Are there any foods and beverages consumed while smoke? Why? • Are you able to smoke at home? Why or why not? • Are your parents aware of your smoking?
	2. To what extent have the smoking activities affected their health? 2.1 Have there been attempts to quit smoking?	• How is your health in relation to this addictive activity? • Do you ever plan to quit smoking?

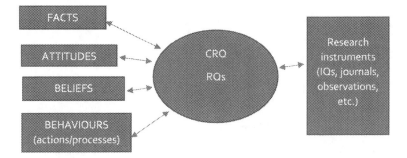

Figure 2.2: An Overview of Facts, Attitudes, Beliefs, and Behaviours (FABB) in Guiding the Formation of CRQs and RQs

In a nutshell, researchers must prepare the right kind of instrument for each of the research questions and conduct a pilot study to test the rigour of the IQs in generating rich information that would explain the RQs and the CRQ. The FABB, as in figure 2.2, is a guiding tool to trigger more ideas as well as evaluate the quality of the interview questions in eliciting in-depth information in explaining the phenomenon. In this context there is an element of iteration from drafting, piloting, and redrafting to finalising the research tools or instruments.

Summary of All Steps (Table 2.1.1)

The need to see the good fit factor across the five constructs (see figure 2.3 below) is paramount in ensuring credible findings. The students must be able to see a helicopter view (see figure 2.2 above) of the entire research. This would avoid being carried away or derailed in the process of understanding the objectives of the research and collecting the necessary data seen fit for the phenomenon. In fact, it is common amongst novice researchers to change the research topics and purposes after piloting activities or preliminary engagement with the informants in the course of building the instruments in the field. Again, it must be remembered that the intent is to explore, understand, and explain a central phenomenon and not just reporting a consensus of the phenomenon. Thus, changing the topic or issue would still require them to maintain the good fit of the five basic constructs, as illustrated in figure 2.3:

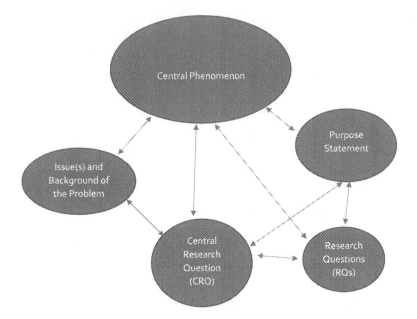

**Figure 2.3: Maintaining the Good Fit of Five
Fundamental Constructs in Qualitative Research**

In figure 2.3, the central phenomenon comprises the statement of purpose and its corresponding background of the problem, purpose statement, CRQ and RQs. The arrows show the interconnectedness of the contents of the four blue ovals. In a sense, the central phenomenon must be represented clearly under the heading of "Background of the Problem" and should be written in the form of Central Research Question (CRQ). A CRQ must be represented by the purpose statement of the entire study and translated into a number of RQs seen crucial in seeking the proper information to explain the phonomenon. In general, there should be a good fit across the five blue ovals before embarking on the research activities. The following are examples of the central phenomenon:

- cultural shock amongst international students at IIUM (concept); and

- the process of understanding and using Malay language amongst new international undergraduate students (process),

What is the purpose of research? It is a statement of an overall focus and direction of the concept, such as to explore the experiences of cigarette smoking amongst female students in a private secondary school in Kuala Lumpur.

The central question (CQ), or central research question (CRQ), as used by the author intends to open the corridors for the informants to share their perspectives and not focus purely on the researchers' perspectives. So it is always written as generally as possible to capture the essence of conducting the study.

Writing a good CQ would require three basic elements: the central phenomenon, the participants/informants, and the research site (Creswell 2012).

The CQ/CRQ may be supported by a number of issues and procedural subquestions. Normally, the subquestions would focus on specific issues and procedural matters. As an example of a CQ/CRQ and its subquestions on a particular issue:

- What is the examination for primary school pupils in a private tuition centre in Kuala Lumpur? (CQ/CRQ)
  - What is private tuition to the pupils? (subquestion)
  - How do the pupils relate tuition to academic success? (subquestion)
  - How do the pupils cope with the private tutors? (subquestion)
  - What is the examination for the pupils' family? (subquestion)

Thus, the guiding principle of conducting qualitative research should take into account the fundamental interconnectedness or good fit of the above five basic constructs (figure 2.3).

The following table 2.1.1 transforms the constructs in figure 2.3 into practical application, which is based on a proposed qualitative project by one of the postgraduate students supervised by the author many years ago.

Table 2.1.1: An Example of a Summary Flow Process from Issue to IQs

Appendix 16: CRQ, RQs and IQs

Teachers' Perceptions on Attitudes and Motivation toward Learning the English Language
among Students from Islamic Education System Background

ISSUE	CENTRAL PHENOMENON	PURPOSE STATEMENT	CENTRAL RESEARCH QUESTION (CRQ)	RESEARCH QUESTIONS (Subquestions)	INTERVIEW QUESTIONS (IQs)
Attitudes and Motivation	The attitudes and motivation of students from Islamic education system background toward learning English as a second language	The purpose of this qualitative study will be to explore the attitudes and motivation of students from Islamic background from the perspectives of 3 English language teachers at a tertiary institution.	What are the perceptions of English teachers toward attitudes and motivation in learning English as a second language among students from Islamic education background?	1. What are the teachers' understandings of 'attitude' in learning English as a second language among students from Islamic education background?	1. What does 'attitude' in the context of learning an L2 mean to you? 2. Generally, what are your students' attitudes toward learning English? 3. Do you think that your students like English lessons? Why? 4. Do they work hard in English lessons? 5. How do they view the English language?
				2. What are the teachers' understandings of 'motivation' in learning English as a second language among students from Islamic background?	1. What does 'motivation' in the context of learning an L2 mean to you? 2. Do you think that your students are motivated to learn English? Why? 3. What motivates students to learn English?
				3. How do the teachers manage	1. How do you manage / handle students' with

Source: Project Report by Hazlina Abdullah for Advanced Qualitative Research Methods Course (EDF 7810), Kulliyyah of Education, IIUM)

Table 2.1.1 consists of six columns comprising the five constructs discussed and the relevant corresponding interview questions (IQ) for each of the RQs. The order of the six columns is from the general issue on the far left to the specific IQ on the far right. The table would allow the researchers to plot and evaluate whether there is a good fit amongst the five major constructs and the relevant IQs. This simple flow-process table acts as a summary of the research proposal. In fact, an additional column on Methods of Collecting Qualitative

Data can be inserted to the right of the RQs column. Again, each RQ may need one or more method of qualitative data collection such as individual interviews, focus groups, or observations. Yet the researchers must always be critical as to what types of data seem suitable enough to provide an explanation to each of the RQs.

In the case of table 2.1.1, the construction of the IQs for each of the RQs should take into account the following three points:

- The IQs must be the key questions able to extract information seen necessary to explain the phenomenon;
- The IQs must be clear enough to be understood by the informants/respondents; and
- The IQs must be adequate for each of the RQs.

At this juncture all of the IQs are the major guiding questions posed to all of the identified informants. All of the IQs must be asked, and in certain circumstances the researchers may conduct probing questions to elicit further clarification. It is not necessary to write additional probing IQs for each IQ.

2.4 Step 4—Piloting the Interview Questions

Novice investigators may face some challenges in conducting an interview. Frequently, questioning may lead to uneasiness or nervous feelings. Probing questions may feel awkward and intrusive on private matters. Piloting the interview would be a good avenue to develop the researcher's confidence and experience with the interviewees or informants. Essentially, piloting the designed interview questions can be seen as a trial run in checking the feasibility of the IQs, as well as the RQs, and considered crucial because it provides valuable insight for the researchers in improving the quality of the IQs. Besides that, conducting a pilot interview can provide invaluable information as to behaviours, norms, and cultures of targeted informants.

Doing a pilot study may lead to the refinement of interview questions, an orientation towards facing informants, and the minimising of any discomfort or pain in conducting the interview. Piloting may also highlight certain threats to the data-collecting activities such as reluctance and discomfort towards the IQs, the suitability of the IQs language level, and the potential of the IQs in fulfilling the needs of the RQs.

Upon completion of a pilot interview, the researcher may delete, edit, or add interview items accordingly to strengthen the overall interview process and increase its potential of collecting data. Difficult or ambiguous questions must be improved to ensure comprehensibility, whilst in some cases the researchers may need to re-pilot the IQs to assure that they are credible enough prior to collecting the real data. Information from the piloting activity may also be valuable towards adjusting or improving the RQs. The progressive nature of qualitative research is open to the idea that the pilot data can be utilised to provide supportive information for the main study.

In summary, this chapter explores the processes involved in preparing a fundamental qualitative research proposal beginning from a selected issue, central phenomenon, purpose statement, central question (CQ), research questions (RQs), and corresponding interview questions (IQs). The necessary steps are explained, and related examples are attached in the appendixes. The content in this chapter is a precursor to more challenging steps in chapter three.

Chapter 3

Fundamental and Systematic Flow of Generating Quality Qualitative Data: From Piloting to Data Analyses

Patience and perseverance have a magical effect before
which difficulties disappear and obstacles vanish
—John Quincy Adams

This chapter discusses the basic steps and processes involved in collecting, analysing, and generating the main ideas and themes from qualitative data. Due to the many types of qualitative data, the discussion of this chapter focuses on collecting, analysing, and reporting interview data only. The analyses are based on systematic steps that are seen as crucial and important in generating the findings or themes of the research. It is bottom up in approach as well as systematic, labour-intensive, rigorous, and time-consuming, yet it will allow for a comprehensive set of themes to be discovered. Bear in mind that the meaning of credibility and trustworthiness of the findings is a reflection of the rigorousness of the data analyses in assuring that no main ideas are overlooked or swept under the carpet.

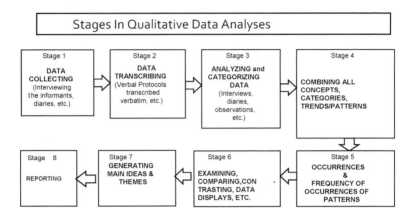

**Figure 3.0—Stages in Qualitative Data
Collection, Analyses, and Reporting**

Figure 3.0 shows the flow of the basic stage and categorizing data involved in conducting a qualitative research: collecting data, transcribing data, analysing, generating themes, and reporting the qualitative data. The following is a discussion on the stages involved as depicted in figure 3.0 above.

3.1 Stage 1—Collecting Qualitative Data

There are many types of qualitative data, such as participant and non-participant observations, a record of personal experiences or diaries, documents, and interviews. In all circumstances the researcher must first determine the suitable sites and participants or informants relatable to the observed phenomenon that can provide rich data in explaining the issue raised in the CRQ prior to the data collecting activities.

Upon identification of a suitable site, several actions should be taken to ensure that data is gained ethically and accountably as it will enhance the credibility and trustworthiness of the study. The fundamental actions to be taken in stage 1 include the following:

- Rich data identifies the site and informants that can provide the richest information required in explaining the phenomenon raised in the CRQ. Usually, the best place would be wherever the phenomenon is seen as occurring.
- Sampling: Decide the best sampling type in identifying the informants – purposive, snowball sampling, or both? In any case, the researcher must understand the strengths and weaknesses of the sampling technique used.
- Gatekeepers: The authorities managing the site should be approached for permission to enter and conduct the research within their area of jurisdiction. A letter of reference from your agency along with any approved grant letters or documentations should be presented to the site's authorities to gain access. A consent letter or verbal approval from the people in charge of the research site should first be gained before entering the site as a researcher. This is useful as the gatekeepers/information providers normally assist in many aspects of the data collection, such as identifying the right informants, clearing the air regarding the intention of the study, and matters on confidentiality of the research findings.
- Prepare for the interview: This involves identifying a suitable setting with few or no distractions. For a novice researcher, it is important to practice mock interviews, taking into consideration a proper unstressed environment or setting, which would encourage openness and increase the potential of tapping richer information. In any circumstance, attending basic training on how to conduct a successful interview would help.
- Recording devices: Digital voice recorders and smartphones are used to record conversations. Always check the functionality of the devices as well as be familiar with them. Extra batteries are certainly needed. Through experience, it is better to utilize at least two recording devices at the same time: each would back up the other in case one of the devices

is faulty. Some digital voice recorders have a voice-operated recording (VOR) function that will automatically record when sound is detected. The risk of this function is that the device may fail to record if the voice of the conversation is too soft or low. Thus, it is advisable the VOR function is switched off, which would allow continuous recording in order to capture all sounds as much as possible. In some cases parts of the interview are deemed too sensitive to the informants to be recorded. Pause the recording, and after the interview take note of the key ideas of the sensitive parts. Remember, making an appointment with the informant is not an easy matter, so make it a worthy occasion.

- Remembering key interview questions: Conduct the interview in a casual manner and avoid being too formal or rigid. It is better to remember or note down the keywords for each interview question, which trigger the question to be asked. Remember, an interview is a conversation with a purpose, and it may not be possible to ensure that the informants adhere to the flow of the interview questions. Always encourage the informants to speak and do some digging of information until you are satisfied with the responses and no further information could be elicited. This is known as reaching the saturation point.

- Rights of the informants: With respect of the informants, it is only appropriate that the individuals selected are given a proper explanation about the intention of the research and an informed consent (see appendixes 1a and 1b) is received as a proof that they are willing to participate in the interview. The informants should be informed of the confidentiality of the information and their rights to share or withhold certain information. They must be aware that they have that freedom to withdraw from the interview if they feel the need to do so.

3.2 Stage 2—Organising the Qualitative Data for Analyses – Data Transcribing

Organizing qualitative data is a fundamental step prior to any analysis. Any materials collected, such as interviews, observations, documents, and visual materials must be systematically categorized, kept, and documented for easy retrieval.

For an interview, data from various informants must be transcribed verbatim and a notational convention should be developed to guide the interpretation of the codes displayed in the transcripts. The notational convention would serve as a guide to the level of detail representation of the recorded voice. In studies involving linguistic matters such as the pitch of the voice, volume, and intonation of speech, the convention is critical in representing the recorded paralinguistic elements and later interpreting them accordingly.

As an example, the following table 3.0 represents a basic template for transcribing an interview (see appendix 2 for a further example):

Table 3.0: A Basic Transcribing Template

Interview Transcription
Informant: Student 1 Place: Café, K. L. Date: 31 August 2015 Time: 2.30 p.m. – 4 p.m.

Discourse Unit (DU)	R: Researcher I: Informant	Transcription	Remark
1	R	Assalamu'alaikum, brother. How are you this afternoon?	

2	I	Wa'alaikumsalam ... eehh, pretty good. Well, I am a bit nervous you know, but I am ready and willing to share my opinion and experience regarding the issue ehhh ...	-Uneasiness -Motivated
3	R	Ooh great. Remember the day I called you? What do you mean by the term mmm "*tak kisah*" used by your senior supervisor?	
4	I	You see, he is willing to help the trainees well ummm but could not lend his support in cases involving ...	

The following terms, as used in table 3.0, are defined here.

Informant

Maintaining and protecting the real identity of the respondent's or informant's confidentiality – also known as internal confidentiality (Tolich 2004) in qualitative research – is very important and is based on the agreed terms of reference between the researcher and the respondent. However, deductive disclosure of the findings would likely reveal the background and identity of the informant. Since deductive disclosure is a delicate matter, it is recommended that reading the works of Baez (2002), Allen (1997), and Sieber (1992) would heighten the researcher's knowledge and awareness on this matter. In the context of transcribing the interview, a pseudonym is recommended, which will protect the real identity of or provide anonymity for the respondent. In this case, assigning a number, an alias, or any other code would protect the identity of the informant.

Place, Date, and Time

The place, date, and time of the interview should be stated. The place should not be revealed without the consent of the informant. The interviewer may record place, date, and time as "unspecified" if the data is judged to be revealing and may lead to a later potential threat.

Discourse Unit (DU)

Any utterance that contains a discourse entity can be considered as an utterance unit or discourse unit (DU). Any partial utterance without any discourse entity, or a meaningless entity such as an incomplete sentence, is not considered a discourse unit. Thus, the term is meant for meaningful sentences or utterances thought to represent embedded meaningful ideas. The researcher must decide whether a partial or incomplete utterance is meaningful before assigning a DU to it. For example, an informant would say "eaaaa mmm" as a response to a particular question. The expression "eaaaa mmm", coupled with the tone, could be interpreted as being uncertain and avoiding giving the required information. In this case, it is a DU by itself. Transcribing an interview using meaningful units, such as the DUs, serves as a referencing point of support in discussing a particular idea, vignette, or theme. For example, the researcher may want readers to refer to a DU as a source of reference in supporting or highlighting a particular idea or theme in light of debating a particular theory or forwarding a new concept.

If the research touches sensitive issues or is categorized as sensitive research, such as private and sacred matters of a particular individual or group, then a decision has to be made to protect the uttered phrases or words that may later pose a risk to the informant. For example, some specific terms like the word mosque (Muslims' place of prayer) or synagogue (a Jewish place of worship) may risk revealing the religion of the informant. In some cases, the informant may want the researcher to pause the recording device when reporting the sensitive matters. In this case it is wise to recall the information in the post-interview stage and perhaps assign a particular notation, such as ****, for example, to indicate the part of the text being deleted due to its sensitivity. The sensitive DUs may not appear in the transcription, and the researcher must be aware of the context of the sensitive parts in the transcription. As a suggestion, assigning a code of reference to the sensitive parts would help the researcher to recall the context of the conversation. The important thing in undertaking sensitive research is to protect the interest and safety of all parties involved, thus minimizing risk (McCosker, Barnard, and Gerber 2001).

Verbatim Transcription

The trustworthiness of the interview transcripts would add quality and rigour to the qualitative research itself (Poland 1995; Davidson 2009). In this column, the best strategy is to listen to the recorded conversation and convert the conversation into text exactly as it is uttered. This is known as verbatim transcription. In other words, type the recorded sound or audio as best as possible. This requires the transcriber to pay attention to the spoken words. This may include pauses and other non-linguistic utterances such as "eeeaa", a long silence, cynical laughter, or coughing. A lot of patience and time are required in producing a true quality verbatim account. It is wise to transcribe as much as possible the non-verbal communication as well as laughter, fillers like "mmm", "you know", and "aha", and false starts such as "I mean it is …", as these provide rich information to the reasoning and thinking behaviours of the informant.

Avoid paraphrasing because it is not what was uttered by the informant (Poland 1995). Once the transcription is completed, listen again to the recorded audio and check the transcription for added or missing words. A missing word may lead to improper interpretation later. All the codes used in the transcription must be defined in the notational convention of the transcription.

There is software available online, such as Cool Edit Pro 2.1 and Express Scribe that can assist the transcribing process. These programs provide features such as slowing down the speed of the conversation, pausing, and minimizing the background noises. There are other observable matters during the interview, such as non-linguistic elements, body language, and physical appearance, which can be noted in a diary. The information would be useful later in describing related ideas or themes. Please see appendix 2 as an example of a full transcription. The transcription is colour-coded based on the interview questions for ease of reference.**Remark**

More often than not, the researcher will recall and reflect on many aspects of the transcription. It may be in the form of comments, additional information such as thoughts from other studies, new ideas, or the meaning of specific terms in the context of the conversation. This column allows the researcher to recall, reflect, and link other noted observations for that particular DU. In some cases it allows reinterpretation of the main ideas of the DUs and sensitive issues that are not recorded but raised in the diary. It can serve as a cross-referencing tool to related literature reviews, theories, diaries, documents, and other means of recorded data.

Table 3.1—Notational Conventions: Symbols and Abbreviated Expressions

Symbol/Abbreviation	Meaning
R	Researcher
I	Informant
//..... //	simultaneous utterances by the researcher and informant
*	ill-formed utterances
..	Each dot indicates a pause of one second. In this case, it is a two-second pause.

In the above discussion, the terms notational convention or notation system connotes the meaning of notation in the form of symbols and abbreviations used throughout the transcription. A known conversation analysis (CA) convention that serves as a guide is by Gumperz and Berenz (1993). As an example, table 3.1 (above) represents a notational convention used in explaining the meaning of the symbols and abbreviations used in a transcription (Ismail Sheikh Ahmad 1997). Each symbol and abbreviation must be defined accordingly in clarifying its contextual meaning in a transcription. The same convention must be used throughout all transcripts to ensure a standard interpretation of the meaning of each symbol or abbreviation.

3.3 Stage 3—Analysing and Categorizing the Transcribed Data: Generating Main Ideas

There are many ways to analyse the transcribed data. The following discussion focuses on theme-generating techniques. There are a number of fundamental steps in analysing the transcribed data (see table 3.2 below):

- Read each transcription carefully. Normally, the IQs asked would be in a sequence, from RQ1 to the final RQ. However, more often than not the informant may express related ideas to each IQ not in any particular sequence. For example, it is possible that an informant would provide particular information to IQ1 as well as link the explanation with the needed information in IQ15. In another scenario, the explanation for IQ12 touches some related information pertinent to IQs 6 and 7, respectively. It must be remembered that an informant or respondent should be allowed to share information as much as possible, and the interviewer should know what kind of information is shared and whether the information has reached the saturation point before shifting to the next question.

  At this juncture, it must be remembered that an interview is a conversation with a purpose (Burgess 1984), and the interviewer must be alert to the IQs that have not been responded to adequately. In a nutshell, an idea or information to a particular IQ may appear in different parts of the transcription. One of the best ways to detect and capture the related information to each IQ is by assigning a specific colour code to the information related to each IQ. Thus, the researcher must colour the contextualised phrases or words as belonging to a particular RQ observed throughout the transcription. Thus, there could be more than a dozen colours used in a text. In the past, the author used to cut the related phrases or words to each IQ and arrange them accordingly for later coding.

- Once the colour coding activity is done, the next step is to transfer the selected ideas (the colour-coded phrases or words) into a template named Generating Main Ideas, as seen in table 3.2 (see appendix 3). It must be remembered that each template belongs to a set of interview transcription only.

Table 3.2—Coding Template for Generating Main Ideas

Appendix 8 : Coding for I1

Generating Main Ideas

Informant 1 (I1)

1	2	3	4	5	6	7
INTERVIEW QUESTIONS	SUPER-ORDINATE Keywords of the Questions	SUB-ORDINATE Main Points from Conversation (Not a summary)	ELABORATION Examples from verbal to support the sub-ordinate	OCCURRENCE Main ideas transferred as keyword(s) based on summary of the sub-ordinate facts (3)	FREQUENCY OF OCCURRENCE	ORDERING OF DISCOURSE UNIT
1. What does 'attitude' in the context of learning an L2 mean to you?	'attitude' learning an L2	- attitudes covers everything —	- students' interests em towards language learning, and then their anticipation, their learning habits, emm err their participation in class. - their long-term goals, for me that is, that includes their attitudes or reflect their attitudes	Interests Anticipation Learning habits Class participation Long-term goals		18
2. Generally, what are your students' attitudes toward learning English?	your students' attitudes	- I would say my students err have, have the interest to learn the language, to be proficient in that language ... but I would say the motivation is	- ...they want English for academic purposes but not for survival. So I would say the success rate or the attitude is slightly different. - The motivation is not that strong. They want to pass, they want to learn err maybe because they want to pass.	To pass examination		20 , 22, 30

The following discussion elaborates on the information in table 3.2. The table is a partial section of a complete set but adequate to guide the discussion. A sample of a complete set generating the main ideas can be seen in appendix 2.

Interview Questions (Column 1)

Each interview question must be written accordingly. It is not the uttered interview questions as transcribed but the standard interview questions as stipulated in the interview protocol. The same official or formal interview questions should be maintained throughout the other coding templates. As an example (see table 3.2), interview question number 1, "What does 'attitude' in the context of learning an L2 mean to you?", is the standard interview question used and will remain unchanged in the similar coding template for the other informants interviewed and responded to the oral questions on the same topic.

Superordinate (Column 2)

This column requires the keywords or gist of the interview questions. In the case of interview question number 1 (see table 3.2 above), the keywords and key phrases are *attitude* and *learning a second language or L2*. This helps the researcher to focus on the key points of each of the interview questions.

Subordinate (Column 3)

At this juncture, highlight the key points or main ideas of the conversation that responded to each interview question. The highlighted main ideas must be *the uttered words or phrases or sentences thought to represent the responses to each interview question as verbalised in the transcription and should not be a summary of the ideas.* Remember, the responses may appear in different parts of the text. So it is suggested that assigning a specific colour code or highlighting the key uttered ideas may be useful in assuring a systematic analysis of the transcription.

Let us say the key uttered main ideas for IQ1 would be colour-coded light green. Thus, light green may appear in different parts of the transcription which represents verbalized ideas to interview question number 1. The researcher must read the transcription carefully and highlight any words or phrases thought or interpreted to represent information to IQ1. Thus, information for IQ8 may appear in DUs of IQ12.

Thus, reading the transcription carefully would highlight contextualized interpretation of the main ideas occurring in various discourse units (DUs). In table 3.2, the uttered main idea *attitudes cover everything* in responding to interview question 1 was only observed once as shown in DU 16 and not in any other discourse unit read. In other words, there are cases whereby a number of uttered main ideas may appear in different parts of each transcription. So the researcher must be cognisant of this situation and highlight them using the same colour coding for each interview question. The reason for this is the fact that an informant may respond to a question in a recursive manner and thus the ideas may be interpreted as having direct and indirect connection to a particular research question.

Each main idea in column 3 should be bulleted and should correspond to the supported examples, if any (column 4).

Elaboration (Column 4)

An informant may provide examples in explaining the main ideas. The interviewer should be fully engaged in the conversation and probing deeper as to the why and how of the main ideas, which would allow rich or thick information in explaining the main ideas. The illustrations or examples for each main idea may appear in different parts of the text. Thus, each main idea in column 3 may be supported by a number of examples appearing in different parts of the transcription.

Occurrence of Main Ideas and Frequency of Occurrence (Columns 5 and 6)

Technically, column 5 represents the summarized main ideas for all of the uttered main ideas in column 3. To be more specific, each main idea in column 3 must be summarized into a meaningful contextualized main idea in column 5. There may be a repeated main idea by the same informant, and it is advised that the same main idea be recorded because it shows the degree of concern of the informant for that particular IQ. Thus, each main idea (uttered as in column 3) must be summarized in column 5, regardless of how many times the same main idea appears in responding to the individual interview question.

For example, let us assume that the summarised "to pass examination" (see table 3.2, IQ 2, column 5) appears three times as represented in the relevant subordinate idea (column 3). Thus, the frequency of occurrence (column 6) for "to pass examination" is three times, and later, when coupled with the other informants for the same IQ, "to pass examination" could add up to more than three times. If frequency of occurrence is used to explain the meaning of IQ1, then out of the total main ideas for IQ1 for all informants, the researcher would be able to calculate the percentage of "to pass examination" out of the total main ideas for IQ1. In a simple manner, a repeating main idea connotes a major concern of the informants for a particular IQ.

Ordering of Discourse Unit (DU) in Column 7

It is important to note down or locate the reference for each of the main ideas and elaboration in column 7. This would assist the researcher to locate the specific DUs faster and recall the context of the conversation without reading the entire transcription repeatedly. It helps others, such as the examiners, to understand the context of the conversation leading to naming the related themes as written in the research report. It also serves as a source of reference, such as the relevant quotes and in interpreting and supporting the meaning of each theme later on. A verbalised idea may not be expressed in a single DU. Normally, it involves a number of DUs and is important to highlight the DUs, such as 20–28. In this case, DUs 20–28 means the conversation pertaining to the idea is captured between DUs between twenty and twenty-eight times in the transcription.

3.4 Stage 4—Combining Main Ideas in Generating Themes

Table 3.3 Coding Templates for Generating Themes

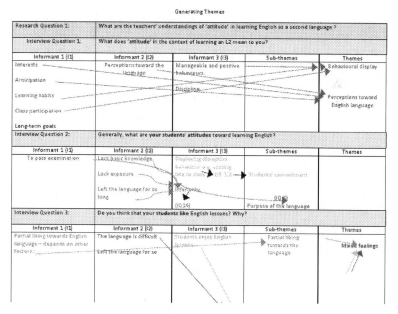

The ultimate journey in analysing the data is to answer the research questions. Creswell (2012 247–8) highlighted that

> Describing and developing themes from the data consists of answering the major research questions and forming

> an in-depth understanding of the central phenomenon through description and thematic development [and] themes have labels that typically consist of no more than two or four words (e.g. 'denial', 'campus planning').

The fundamental question is how to generate the themes? Generating themes is a recursive process requiring a critical mind in making sense of the data. The following discussion illustrates the processes in generating the themes that would subsequently explain the CRQ or the central phenomenon under investigation.

Table 3.3 serves as a general and fundamental template in generating themes (see appendix 4 for other examples). Table 3.3 is inductive in nature where the generated main ideas are being critically narrowed to a number of themes.

There are five columns in table 3.3. In the first three columns, Informant 1, Informant 2, and Informant 3. The main ideas are listed based on the generated main ideas from column 5 in table 3.2. The researcher must remember the key point here: the many main ideas uttered by the informants in column 5 (table 3.2) must be interpreted and transformed as themes. There could be several main ideas representing a single theme *or* a number of themes. In this case, the interpreted main ideas thought to represent a similar theme are assigned a specific colour. Assigning a specific colour code would assist in generating the themes systematically. Column 4 is meant for subthemes. There is a possibility that a particular major theme can be best illustrated by a number of subthemes. In other words, the subthemes elaborate the major theme more clearly, and it depends on the interpretation of the main ideas.

In column 5, titled Themes, as in table 3.3, the blue and red arrows for IQ1 represent a group of main ideas ("What does 'attitude' in the context of learning an L2 mean to you?"), which were critically interpreted and thought to represent two themes: Behavioural Display, and Perceptions of English Language, respectively.

The same step of grouping the main ideas should be done for the remaining interview questions. There might be situations where a main idea stands alone. In this case it can be a theme by itself, as there could be a situation whereby a main idea was judged to fit as a theme due to its representativeness of the ideas of the IQ even though it was mentioned only once by an informant throughout the interview. This is acceptable as the process of coding in qualitative research is aimed at reducing repetition or redundancy of assigned "codes" or main ideas in the development of themes.

3.5 Stage 5—Reliability in Qualitative Research: Credibility/Trustworthiness of the Generated Themes

The quality or the worthiness of the generated themes must be screened accordingly. In light of this, Lincoln and Guba (1985) posit the term trustworthiness or the extent to which a person can trust or believe the findings of the study (Glaser and Strauss 1967), which includes the elements of credibility, transferability, dependability, and confirmability in evaluating the findings.

Credibility reflects the notion of confidence in the findings. As an example, if the study generates a theoretical or conceptual framework, it must be based on the proper interpretation of the data. In other words, the explanation of the theoretical model or framework must be clear and supported with the available evidence from the data. It is also important to understand the concept of theoretical saturation of data whereby the study has reached a point of no new information for the research questions based on the data gathered from the field (Seale 1999). In a sense, there seems to be more or less similar themes or categories found after the sampling and interpretation activities, thus leading to the point where the themes or categories could not be further developed. Once saturation point is reached, the researcher can show confidence in finalizing his or her analysis and forward the theoretical model or framework in explaining the studied phenomenon.

Transferability is a concept of the applying or transferring the findings to other similar contexts. Thus, the conclusions of the study can be transferred to other settings or situations or perhaps times.

Transferability is always associated with the contextualized thick description of the field experiences (Holloway 1977).

Dependability connotes the consistency of the findings of similar studies being repeated in similar settings. One of the ways to establish dependability is through external auditors, who evaluate the research's findings, data analyses, and explanations, as well as generated theories or models, whether or not they are well justified by the data (Creswell 1998; Lincoln and Guba 1985; Miles and Huberman 1994).

Confirmability reflects the notion of being unbiased in telling the truth of the findings without any undisclosed interest at all by the researchers. An audit trail, triangulation, or various sources of data and reflexivity are some of the techniques establishing confirmability or degree of being neutral in reporting the findings.

Table 3.4 (Hazlina Abdullah 2012) serves as a guide in summarizing the generated themes for all of the research questions raised in the study. It helps the researcher to review and critically reflect on the appropriateness of the generated themes or subthemes, if any. If the IQ is related to "how" or involving steps or processes of an event, the likely themes would be action-oriented. In a sense, the table helps in checking the good-fit of the generated themes with the corresponding IQ. Table 3.4 helps the researcher to check the possibilities that the generated themes or categories could be further fine-tuned due to choice of words or phrases in reflecting the generated main ideas and the subsequent themes. Other examples in summarising the generated themes can be referred to in appendix 5.

Table 3.4A—Summary of the Generated
Themes by RQ and IQs

Appendix 11 (b)

Generated Themes and Sub-themes

Research question 1: What are the teachers' understandings of 'attitude' in learning English as a second language	
Interview question 1: What does 'attitude' in the context of learning an L2 mean to you?	
Sub-themes	Themes
	• Behavioural display • Perceptions toward English language

Interview question 3: Do you think that your students like English lessons? Why?	
Sub-themes	Themes
• Partial liking towards the language • English is difficult • English lessons are enjoyable	• Mixed feelings

Interview question 5: How do they view the English language?	
Sub-themes	Themes
• Difficulty of the language • Relevancy of the language • Lack of basic knowledge • Nationalistic reason • Religious reason	• Negativity towards the language
• English for work purposes • English for exam purposes	• Purpose of the language
• Opening up towards the language	• Paradigm shift

Research question 2: What are the teachers' understandings of 'motivation' in learning English as a second language?	
Interview question 6: What does 'motivation' in the context of learning an L2 mean to you?	
Sub-themes	Themes
	• Intrinsic motivation • Extrinsic motivation

A template to summarize the generated subthemes and themes is shown in table 3.4 (Hazlina Abdullah 2012). There are slots where the subthemes are generated as well as not generated at all due to the availability and interpreted information in the transcription. For example, for RQ1 alone, the IQ3 produces three subthemes later interpreted as belonging to a major theme named "mixed feelings". In the case of RQ2, there are no generated subthemes for IQ6 but two themes named "intrinsic motivation" and "extrinsic motivation". As a reflection, deep probing is crucial in explaining a particular event, and this would certainly be affected by the informants' willingness to reflect and the alertness of the interviewers in data saturation. However, naming or assigning a theme is not an easy process. The researchers must interpret the context of the conversation and create a theme judged suitable for the uttered information based on the given interview question.

3.6 Stage 6—Inter-Rater Reliability Check on Thematic Coding

Generating the main ideas or themes is not an easy task, and thus themes generated would empower the analysis and conclusion of the study (Miles and Huberman 1994). On top of the depth and breadth of discussion in explaining the themes of the phenomenon under study, the credibility of the generated codes or themes could be enhanced through an inter-reliability check. This would certainly add rigour to the generated data. Not all qualitative data must undergo inter-rater or intercoder reliability checks.

The focus of the following discussion is centred on themes generated from in-depth semi-structured interviews as illustrated in table 3.5. Here, the focus is on agreement amongst the raters for selected sets of coded themes by the researcher. The purpose of the inter-rater reliability check is to allow the raters to rate their agreement for a set of themes selected at random across the RQ and IQ.

An inter-rater should not be confused with an intercoder. The former is concerned with the generated themes produced by the researchers; the raters' main task is to rate "agree" or "disagree" on each theme and suggest improvements. The latter is concerned with reproducibility across coders. The same set of rated themes by the raters can be given to the coders. Thus, comparison on the agreement, using the formula in table 3.6, can be made between the raters and the coders.

Would the different coders similarly code the same set of data? In this context, the themes generated by the researcher are not shared with the coders. The coders are given a set of data, such as a selected interview transcription from the various interview questions, and their main task is to generate appropriate themes out of the transcriptions. Later, the coders' generated themes are compared with the researcher's coded themes and rated in terms of the agreement of the themes between the coder's and the researchers', as formulated by Miles and Huberman (1994) as

Reliability = number of agreements divided by total number of agreements plus disagreement

If there are two or more coders, the average percentage of agreement must be calculated across the number of coders. Agreement consistency in the range of 90 per cent and above is judged as good quality rated or coded themes (Miles and Huberman 1994, 64).

As an example in table 3.5, the rater must decide whether the generated main ideas and themes are reasonably done in light of the IQ and RQ. Comments are made in the given column. As a suggestion, the researcher must select a number of IQs from a few RQs and prepare the required materials, as in Table 3.5, to be given to the raters. In the context of the coders, identify 3 to 4 coders who are experts in the same field of study and get their consent to be the coders. Next, teach them the steps taken in generating the themes. The coders should not be influenced to agree with the identified themes but encouraged to be more self-reflective by giving their comments to the themes.

Table 3.5 Inter-Rater Reliability Coding Template

Attitudes and Motivation toward Learning the English Language among Students from Islamic Education System Background:

Exploring the Views of Teachers

Research Question 4:
What are the actions taken by teachers in promoting positive attitudes and motivation to the students?

	Themes	Main Ideas	Verbal Support		Inter-rates		Comments / Suggestions
					Agree	Disagree	
RQ 11: What are the actions that you take in order to instill / inculcate / inspire your students so that they have positive attitudes and high motivation in learning the L2?	Variety of teaching techniques	Online learning	Informant 1 (I1)	online learning web, err I upload on newspaper articles actually almost daily			I will argue that perhaps generally not effective and balanced well to be acceptable
		Use of L1 in	Informant 2 (I2)	In teaching I have to switch using both languages so that they will slowly understand.	✓		
		Teaching materials	Informant 3 (I3)	materials as well, like what I did currently, what I'm doing now... is that I use a newspaper article			
	Words of advice	Advice	Informant 1 (I1)	I told students the more they read, the better they can learn, the faster they can learn...			
		Telling inspirational / personal stories	Informant 2 (I2)	I like to tell them stories of my own personal experience because am, I was also from an religious school...			
		Conveying the importance of English via pep talk	Informant 3 (I3)	I like to give pep (pep) talk	✓		

The University of Auckland

Table 3.6 Inter-Raters' Reliability Calculation

Appendix 14

Calculation of Inter-raters' Reliability

	Percentage (%) of Agreement (Total Number of Agreement / Total Number of Responses) X 100%
Inter-rater 1:	(18 / 18) X 100 = 100%
Inter-rater 2:	(15/18) X 100 = 83.3%
Average:	(33 / 36) X 100 = 91.7%

Formula

In table 3.6, a total of eighteen themes are used by the researcher to be rated by the raters. In this case there are only two identified raters. Rater 1 agreed 100 per cent with the eighteen generated themes, and Rater 2 agreed with only fifteen out of the eighteen, thus calculated as 83.3 per cent. Using Miles and Huberman's formula, the average percentage for both raters' agreement is 92.7 per cent. This is judged as good because the researchers have produced the themes in an objective manner based on the inputs from the collected data. The above procedures, as illustrated in tables 3.5 and 3.6, strengthened the credibility of the coded or rated themes, which is based on the shared constructs, and the conclusions drawn from the data are not overly subjective but scientifically done.

Table 3.7 Audit Trail

Appendix 15 : AUDIT TRAIL

11 September	Selection of Topic Preparing CRQ, RQs and IQs
▼	
27 September 2012	Pilot Interview: *Myra Aldrin, PhD.* *10 years teaching experience*
▼	
10 October 2012	Data Collection *Informant 1 (I1)* *13 years teaching experience*
▼	
12 October 2012	Data Collection *Informant 2 (I2)* *13 years teaching experience* *Informant 3 (I3)* *12 years teaching experience*
▼	
15 – 22 October 2012	Transcription of Data
▼	
23 – 31 October 2012	Analysis of Data : *Coding*
▼	
10 – 29 November 2012	Analysis of Data : *Generating themes and sub-themes*
▼	
1 – 10 December 2012	Inter-rater Reliability *2 Inter-raters*
▼	
Throughout the semester	Reading for Literature Review Multiple Drafts of Written Report
▼	
31 December 2012	Submission of Written Report

Trustworthiness of a qualitative research can be enhanced through an audit trail. It carries the notion of caring and quality assurance, thus establishing confirmability of the research; the research findings from the collected data are systematic, objective, and worthy (Lincoln and Guba 1985; Koch 2006; Sandelowski 1986). An audit trail (see table 3.7; further examples can be seen in appendix 7) shows major activities, steps, and decisions throughout the study kept in a log. The trail provides evidence, normally steps taken, from collecting, analysing, synthesizing, to reporting the data. The audit trail may include data from field notes involving the researchers' observations (see, do, hear, smell, think) noted in a diary, recorded voice, photos, or through any other devices. An audit trail would assist the researchers in reflecting or reviewing the strategies used in data collecting activities and issues faced in conducting the study as well as devising alternative strategies or plans to fulfil the research objectives. Thus, an audit trail is much more than just enhancing the credibility and rigour in the findings alone.

For further reading, there are six categories of data in establishing a well-informed audit trail as discussed by Lincoln and Guba (1985):

1. Raw data;
2. Data reduction and analysis note;
3. Data reconstruction and synthesis products;
4. Process notes;
5. Materials related to intentions and dispositions; and
6. Preliminary development information.

Clearly, being transparent in recording the steps taken in the research activities will add credibility to the research itself. In this context, Malterud says, "Declaring that qualitative analysis was done, or stating that categories emerged when the material had been read by one or more persons, is not sufficient to explain how and why patterns were noticed … the reader needs to know the principles and choices underlying pattern recognition and category foundation" (2001, 486).

In summary, the bulk of this chapter deals with the basic steps and tools in organising, coding, interpreting, and theme generating of the transcribed data. The researchers must be objective in generating the themes, and this is where they must reflect critically in choosing the best words of the themes for each of the research questions. Selected templates are chosen to support the processes at arriving at the proper themes. Fundamental concepts and steps in addressing the credibility and trustworthiness of the generated themes are explained and supported with examples in the appendixes.

Chapter 4

Mechanisms in Reporting Qualitative Research: How and What Should Be Written?

> The worse thing that contemporary qualitative research can imply is that, in this post-modern age, anything goes. The trick is to produce intelligent, disciplined work on the very edge of the abyss.
> —David Silverman, Interpreting Qualitative Data

4.1 Formatting Issues—How Do I Report My Qualitative Data?

Currently there seem to be no clear-cut standard criteria or a single accepted convention for reporting qualitative research findings. A certain type of qualitative research may best be reported in a certain manner due to the overwhelming amount of data, needs of the audience, and scope of the presentation format. In the academic world, the report of the qualitative findings for a postgraduate degree programme may be presented in a traditional thick narrative form following a certain academic research presentation style preferred by the learning institution whilst qualitative research for a private agency may be a brief case study or executive summary focusing on the gist of the findings and suggestions to move forward.

As suggested by Sandelowski (1998), the qualitative researcher should decide on the best way of telling his or her story depending on the research purpose, type of data, and audience for the report. Most importantly, the researcher should ensure that the findings are not lost on the audience. Hence, the appropriate writing style, terminology used, and suitable graphics should be employed so that it is helpful towards maximizing the comprehension of the report.

Miles and Huberman (1994, 299–300) outlined several tips on making a qualitative report effective. They are:

- Researchers should avoid lengthy quotes as they may turn out vague and confusing.
- Reporting in the narrative form may be interesting as it would be like a story to the readers.
- Strategize the writing so that it suits the audience and carries impact upon them. The writing could either be aesthetically appealing, scientifically factual, morally inclined, or activist motivating depending to the interest and lean of the audience.

Writing a qualitative research report as an academic writing would comprise the following systematic flow of contents, as seen in Figure 4.1.

Chapter	Contents
1	Introduction, Background of the Study, Problem Statement, Purpose of the Study, Research Question(s), Theoretical and/or Conceptual Framework of the Study, Definitions of Key Terms, Concepts, Underlying Assumptions of the Study, Scope, Limitations/ Delimitations, Significance, and Summary
2	Introduction, Literature Review, Theoretical Foundation, Conceptual Framework Affecting the Study, Summary, and Conclusions

3	Introduction, Research Design and Rationale, Role of the Researcher, Research Methodology, Instrumentation, Pilot Study, Data Analysis Plan and Procedure, Issues on Trustworthiness, Ethical Procedures, and Summary
4	Introduction, Pilot Study's Impact, Setting(s), Demographics, Data Collection, Data Analysis, Evidence of Trustworthiness, Findings (by Research Qs), and Summary.
5	Introduction, Interpretation of the Findings, Limitations of the Study, Recommendations, Implications, and Conclusion

Figure 4.1 Qualitative Writing-Up Checklist

(Adapted from https://www.coursehero.com/file/16337711/qualitative-checklist-030212-1doc/)

The above format (figure 4.1) is a typical organizational flow in presenting a dissertation or thesis. The checklist is a fundamental guide in preparing and presenting your write-up in a logical manner. Each chapter highlights the key items that are seen relevant to be reported. More often than not your research supervisor would assist you as to the best way to report your research findings. It should not be seen as a rigid standardized format in reporting qualitative findings. A journal may prefer a different format of presenting a qualitative report.

This chapter offers a basic understanding of reporting qualitative research as an end product of an academic endeavour and its basic strategic and systematic reporting format. It discusses some fundamental issues and weaknesses in reporting qualitative findings (as observed by the author in reviewing many qualitative research theses and dissertations) that the writers should bear in mind. Amongst them are

- Heavy reliance on themes and quotes in analysing and reporting the data;

- Weak mechanisms in analysing the qualitative data;
- Discussing the themes in silos;
- Lacking interconnection amongst the themes;
- Lacking in-depth discussion or thick description on themes; and
- Weak themes due to lack of in-depth probing techniques (barely scratching the surface).

Inundating the report with themes and weak interconnectedness amongst the themes in building concepts or models are some of the problems observed in journal articles (Bazeley 2009). In lieu of this, Miles and Huberman (1994, 10–11) highlighted the importance of data displays (matrices, graphs, charts, models, and networks) in guiding the readers, as well as the examiners, to make sense of the massive qualitative data. Data displays add credibility to the emergence of themes and they are a part of data analysis which helps the researcher in simplifying and naming the themes.

The fundamental question raised by my postgraduate students in qualitative report writing is, "What is the best way to effectively report the findings?" There is no warrant for one particular reporting style or strategy. Based on the author's experience in guiding postgraduate students in writing qualitative dissertations and theses, the reporting format taken is more or less the same as in figure 4.1. However, in discussing the findings, it is suggested the themes be presented by following the order of the research questions raised in chapter 1. Thus, the presentation and discussion of the themes should be done by following the sequence of the research questions posed in chapter 1 and in discussing key generated themes.

For example in light of RQ1, the researcher may have many themes to be discussed out of the interview questions and other sources of qualitative data collected. A decision has to be made as to the major salient or best themes that provide sufficient evidence or support from the collected data in explaining the RQ. The themes should engender further discussion on the conceptual or theoretical frameworks mentioned in chapter 1. The generated themes too should provide "answers" to the RQ. In figure 4.2, the researcher may add subthemes in further explaining the related themes. The subthemes provide deeper ideas or characteristics of the themes, allowing for a much richer explanation in justifying the generated themes.

Figure 4.2: An Example of a Matrix Display of a Research Question with the Key Themes

Research Question 1 (RQ1)	What are the teachers' understandings of "attitude" in learning English as a Second Language?
Major themes	• Behavioural display • Paradigm shift • Negativity towards the language

Generally speaking, there are two main approaches to report the qualitative findings: the traditional and the eclectic (Bernard et al. 2008). The former focusses on presenting the themes in isolation without bridging or discussing them with the related studies reported in the literature review in chapter 2, and the latter, usually in a different chapter, gives due emphasis on discussing and connecting the themes with other related studies and the related conceptual and theoretical frameworks mentioned in the first two chapters of the thesis or dissertation.

A typical problem is presenting each theme in a descriptive manner with quotes (and in some cases as much as a page) as a mechanism in explaining the theme. Interestingly enough, the theme could have been a minor one and thus not representing the major ideas of the related data in answering the major issue of the RQ. Furthermore, each of the presented themes is detached from the other themes and there seems to be no interconnectedness or flow of ideas amongst the themes in light of the research question.

4.2—Describe-Compare-Relate (DCR): From Themes to Generating Model/Theory

Bazeley (2009) raised the notion of Garden Path Analysis in describing the action of reporting themes in isolation, lacking interconnection from one another towards answering the CRQ. As a result, the report would lack comprehensiveness and the research findings seem weak. Thus, a formulaic approach of reporting characterised as describe-compare-relate (DCR) is suggested. It is a step-by step guidance in making the presentation of the themes more lively and convergent in nature, leading to a coherent and compact model or theory from the data.

Figure 4.3—Presenting a Theme: Describe-Compare-Relate (Bazeley 2009, 9–10)

Describe	Outline the context for the study and provide details about sources of data, such as the demographic features of the sample and the interrelationships between these features. These give necessary background against which further analyses will be read, as well as providing a basis for comparative analysis. Then move to the first major category or 'theme'. Describe (and record) its characteristics and boundaries. *How* did people talk about this aspect, and *how many* talked about it? What's *not* included?"

Compare	Compare differences in the characteristics and boundaries for just that category or theme across contrasting demographic groups or across variations in context. Do themes occur more or less frequently for different groups? Are they expressed differently by different groups? Ask questions of your data about this category or theme—who, why, what, when? Record meaningful associations—doing so will prompt further questions in your mind. Record, also, an absence of association—not only is it important to know if there is no variation across groups or contexts, recording these means you won't need to waste time later rechecking.
Relate	Relate this category or theme to others already written about. Ask more questions—does it make a difference if …? Use Strauss's (1987) coding paradigm to assist: Under what conditions does this category or theme arise? What actions/interactions/strategies are involved? What are the consequences and do these vary depending on the particular circumstances or the form in which it is expressed? Record the questions you ask, and the results you find (or don't find).

Figure 4.3 summarises the elements of DCR for each theme, as presented by Bazeley (2009, 9–10). DCR would allow the writers to be more grounded to the data, more meaningful and critical in discussing the generated themes, which would subsequently lead to a better proposed concept or theory out of the themes.

In a macro sense, a proposed model comprising themes for each RQ would lead to a collection of models in explaining the issues raised by the RQs as illustrated in Figure 4.4. *The key salient themes would be able to explain the RQ and later lead to constructing a micro-concept or model.* Subsequently, the various micro concepts or models from the various RQs would lead to the formation of a new emerging macro concepts or models answering the CRQ and explaining the phenomenon. The new emerging models or concepts would contribute to the corpus of knowledge in the field leading to a potential theoretical development in light of the existing models and theories in the field, and propel further research activity.

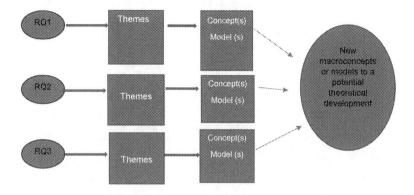

Figure 4.4—From Themes to New Hypothetical Concepts/Models in Theoretical Development

Another perspective in making the discussion more analytical or critical is the notion of emerging divergent views in light of various sources of data (Bazeley 2009; Roller and Lavrakas 2015). The divergent or negative cases or contradictory themes can further explain the phenomenon beyond the identified categories or themes. Contradicting themes emerging from the various data sources would add more dimension and thick explanation to the phenomenon and conclusion of the study. Thus, it serves as a check-and-balance mechanism and trigger more in-depth analysis of why the so-called negative cases or outliers appear in the data and thus producing a more robust analysis of findings. Triangulation of different sources of data and its interpretation by a number of data analysts as well as reflexive journal in reviewing the steps taken in data interpretation would add more breadth and quality in the analysis and in drawing conclusions (Roller and Lavrakas 2015).

Another perspective that would enhance the quality of the analysis is to learn from other analyses drawn from other qualitative studies. Critical reading from other studies, in data analyses and reports, could trigger and relate more ideas in writing up the report (Bazeley 2009).

Displaying the analysed data in an orderly manner helps in describing and explaining the findings accordingly. Miles and Huberman (1994, 91–2) suggest:

> You know what you display. Valid analysis requires, and is driven by, displays that are focused enough to permit a viewing of a full data set in the same location, and are arranged systematically to answer the research questions at hand. A full data set does not, of course, mean the complete field notes. Rather, the condensed, distilled data presented are drawn from the full range of persons, events, and processes under study.

There are no specific rules guiding the format of the displays. The researcher should be creative enough to design reasonable and practical displays that can best explain the findings. Basically, there are two types of displays: matrices (rows and columns) and networks. Matrix displays, flow charts and models, graphs, and typologies are examples of useful supporting displays that can enhance the analyses and reporting of the qualitative findings. See Miles and Huberman (1994, 90–142) for further information.

4.3 Basic Steps in Writing an Effective Discussion-cum-Interpretation on Findings

There are a number of basic objectives in discussing the findings of your research. Other than sharing your views in interpreting the findings in light of the related studies (literature), practices, and theories, it is also pertinent to highlight key implications of the findings in advancing knowledge in the related field and suggestions for future research. The following key points would add value to the discussion or interpretation of the themes:

- Decide on and select key significant themes and arrange the themes accordingly from most important to less important themes to each RQ.

- Decide the style of presenting the themes: traditional or eclectic (Burnard et al. 2008).

- Be critical and in-depth in discussing the themes. See DCR by Bazeley (2009).

- Arrange the discussion of the themes for each RQ; the themes must show interconnectedness as discussed by Bazeley (2009).

- For all intents and purposes, highlight key or novel contributions of the themes in light of the previous studies and related conceptual and theoretical frameworks.

- Explain in what ways the themes extend knowledge (gap-filling) in the discipline based on the related literature review and the referred models and theories.

- Forward new constructs/dimensions/models/theories in the discipline in light of the referred models and theories in the literature review. Using graphical displays would help to explain the new dimensions.

- Always remember to explain the limitations and delimitations (if any) of the study.

This final chapter deals with the basic mechanics in reporting the rich data in a meaningful manner. Describe-compare-relate (DCR) is chosen as a format in reporting the findings in a coherent way. Some basic systematic flow in forwarding new findings of the research, in the form of new macro-concepts or models, were also discussed.

Appendix 1a

Informed Consent Form to Conduct and Record Interview

UNIVERSITI SAINS ISLAM MALAYSIA

This informed consent form is for English language educators at University X, whom are invited to participate in a research entitled "Teachers' Perspectives on Students' Attitudes and Motivation toward Learning the English Language".

Name of Researcher
Hazlina Abdullah
Name of Organization
FPBU, USIM & Institute of Education, IIUM

This Informed Consent Form has two parts:
 • Information Sheet (to share information about the study with you)
 • Certificate of Consent (for signatures if you choose to participate)

You will be given a copy of the full Informed Consent Form

Part I: Information Sheet

Introduction
This is a study of attitudes and motivation of students in learning English as a second language. You are invited to be part of this study. If you have questions, do not hesitate to ask them of me.

Purpose of the research
The attitudes and motivation of students have been extensively discussed in the area of second or foreign language learning. I would like to formally explore these aspects in relation to students from religious school background. I would like to know more about their attitudes and motivation because this knowledge might help us to learn how to better encourage the students in learning the language. I also want to learn about the different ways that teachers employ to help these students.

Type of Research Intervention
This research will involve your participation in an interview session that will take about 45 minutes to 1 hour.

Participant Selection
You are being invited to take part in this research because your vast experience as a teacher can contribute much to the understanding and knowledge of teaching practices.

Voluntary Participation
The choice that you make will have no bearing on your job or on any work-related evaluations or reports. You may change your mind later and stop participating even if you agreed earlier.

Benefits
There will be no direct benefit to you, but your participation is likely to help find out more about how to upgrade the teaching and learning of English in the religious school community.

Confidentiality
Information about you will not be shared with anyone outside the research team. The information gathered will be kept private. Nothing that you say today will be shared with anybody and nothing will be attributed to you by name.

Right to Refuse or Withdraw
This is a reconfirmation that participation is voluntary and includes the right to withdraw. You will

Page 1 of 3

65

Appendix 1a (continued)

Certificate of Consent

I have been invited to participate in this research on attitudes and motivation of students in learning the English language.

I have read the foregoing information, or it has been read to me. I have had the opportunity to ask questions about it and any questions I have been asked, have been answered to my satisfaction. I consent voluntarily to be a participant in this study.

Name of Participant: _____

Signature of Participant: _____

Date: _____

Signature of researcher taking the consent: _____

Date:

Appendix 1b

Informed Consent Form to Conduct and Record Interview

Consent Form

Title of Research:

Understanding repeaters in an ESL writing course: A case study amongst pre-sessional students in IIUM.

Name of researcher: _____

Confidentiality:

The following data will be recorded: Interview.

All data will be coded so that your anonymity will be protected in any research papers and presentations that result from this research.

Record of Consent:

The signature below indicates that you have understood the information about the research. The participation is voluntary but you may not withdraw from the study at any time. You should receive a copy of the consent form. If you have further questions related to this research, please contact the researcher.

Name: _____

Date: _____

Appendix 2

Transcription Based on Interview Questions

Informant: Student2 Date: 15 August 2015 Place: Cafe, KL Time: 9 - 11 p.m.			
D.U	**Code**	**Transcription**	**Remark**
1	I	Just speak a bit loud ya	
2	R	[ok]	
3	I	[ok] so aa before we start aa can you tell me about your name aa and a little bit about yourself.	
4	R	Ok	
5	I	mm	
6	R	my name is xxxxx but aaa most of friends call me xxx aaa maybe they some sometimes they call me xxxxx	
7	I	mm	
8	R	aaa I am from Japan …	
9	I	Ahmm …	
10	R	aa …	
11	I	How old are you?	
12	R	Aaa 21 years old …	

13	I	mm …	
14	R	and …	
15	I	What what course are you doing?	
16	R	[ok]	
17	I	[going] to do?	
18	R	My course I am doing social sciences aa here …	
19	I	Ok …	
20	R	Insyaalah …	
21	I	Alright …	
22	R	aa maybe.	
23	I	Ok now my first question ya …	
24	R	Ya …	
25	I	first of all I am interested to know about aa your background in learning aa writing itself in English?	
26	R	[ya …]	
27	I	[so] so can you tell me how did you learn writing in English aa back in your country when you were in school?	
28	R	Ok, aa I start learning English from the elementary school. So until now it's about aaa 15 years studying [English …]	
29	I	[mm] …	
30	R	but aaa I am not aaa intentionally aaa study aa in how to write but because I always have problems with grammar …	
31	I	[ahmm …]	
32	R	[mostly] grammar but before I came here aaa I mm study in aa some of called the …	
33	I	you	
34	R	Yes?	
35	I	you can speak in malay …	
36	R	Ok …	

37	I	no problem.	
38	R	aaa it's ok. It's a like aaa international language programme …	
39	I	aha	
40	R	I studied there for academic, English for academic purposes …	
41	I	hmm	
42	R	aa it's not really long. Just for three months …	
43	I	so so that will be after your schooling …	
44	R	ya	
45	I	years …	
46	R	after after my schooling years …	
47	I	So ok …	
48	R	I attend this university in xxxxx before I came here …	
49	I	So you went for a short course?	
50	R	Short course …	
51	I	Aha …	
52	Y	Ya …	
53	I	So so when you were back in school …	
54	R	[aha …]	
55	I	[Ya] how was aaa writing in English aa taught to you?	
56	R	[oo not really …]	
57	I	[what kind of things did you do?]	
58	R	not really not intentionally xx (word unclear)	
59		Aha …	
60	R	dze I think I don't know something problem with the curriculum I think …	
61	I	Ahaa so what kind of exercises were given to you?	

62	R	They just aaa like give me the if I study this grammar is like may be past participle …	
63	I	Aha…	
64	R	some kind of it and they give me an example first aa the teacher explained …	
65	I	ahm ahm …	
66	R	to me something aa and she just gave me aa an exercise [that's all …]	
67	I	[aha alright]	
68	R	we never learn how to write like maybe compare and contrast, argumentative essay or [something …]	
69	I	[mm …]	
70	R	or to analyse pie charts …	
71	I	Ahm..	
72	R	anything aa and even I start learning about that from here but Alhamdulillah when I maybe for a short course short course that I took in xxxx aa may be a bit helped me because they teach me about aa English in academic purposes. Aa Alhamdulillah when I came here aa aa at I sit I sat on level six.	
73	I	Aa	
74	R	[aa]	
75	I	[ok] so so basically now that you are already in our system [ya]	
76	R	[ahm]	
77	I	so you have taken our writing course for two times …	
78	R	This [is the second time …]	
79	I	[aa aa I see]	
80	R	aa	
81	I	[for two times]	
82		[I think]	

83	I	So aaa now aaa what would you say aa the main aa differences between aaa they way you learn how to write now in [this university …]	
84	R	[ahm ahm]	
85	I	with the experience when you were back in	
86	R	[xxxx]	
87	I	[in your country?] aa	
88	R	Aaa here I feel lot better but everything changed but in this semester mostly	
89	I	hmmm	
90	R	aa my teacher my lecturer is very good, he drilled [everyone]	
91	I	[mm]	
92	R	write write write because before, I in short the sh.. in the the last short semester	
93	I	mm	
94	R	aa I took also aa aa skill	
95	I	ya	
96	R	writing [skill]	
97	I	[ahmm]	
98	R	the teacher onl.. aa sometimes explaining about the grammar grammar grammar {laugh} aa aa honestly I bored with [that]	
99	I	[hmm]	
100	R	totally bored …	
101	I	Doing grammar but aaa write?	
102	R	Ya but write writing. I need to write …[I need to see]	
103	I	[So so last time?]	
104	R	ya because	
105	I	you just did grammar grammar [grammar]	
106	R	[no no] no no	
107	I	But no writing?	

108	R	aa ok maybe wa 1 hour for grammar [only]	
109	I	[ahm]	
110	R	after that aa writing but because of the short semester is really short [time xx]	
111	I	[aaa that explains]	
112	R	that really make me really need to aa write write [write]	
113	I	[ahm]	
114	R	but yaa aa but it's ok maybe u know {laugh} what aa a bit that maybe disappointing me is I got 5 times because level 6 when I passed, to skill writing 5.5, the band, after that aa last semes the short semester I got 5.5 [again and]	
115	I	[ahm]	
116	R	I made, I took aa the resit examination still 5.5. three times ...	
117	I	So that's quite consistent isn't it?	
118	R	Ya {both I and R laughed} just ...	
119	I	a'a	
120	R	5.5, 5.5 [I don't know ...]	
121	I	[Aa so our] results aa showed that you know it's quite consistent	
122	R	ya	
123	I	ya, so aa [maybe ...]	
124	R	[Alhamdulillah] it's no aa [decreasing]	
125	I	[ya, definitely] definitely. Aa Ok now aa I I am very interested to know about your problems but I will ask you the questions later on.	
126	R	ahmm	

127	I	But for the time being ya, now, aa I I just want to I just want to know your, how do you feel about aaa learning writing itself in English. You know, how do you feel? Feeling can be [happy can be sad aaa..]	
128	R	[Ya sometimes] maybe aa sometimes maybe will be bored	
129	I	ahm	
130	R	that's why maybe you didn't have any idea how to write but actually I enjoyed and especially this time …	
131	I	Wa [why do you enjoy?...]	
132	R	Because I like] the lecturer is very, is like she's on fire to teach every thing, drill and make sure that her students is aaa doing well in writing. Not only band 6 or so-so he, she wants every students aaa at least 7 the band, that's what I like	
133	I	hmm	
134	R	I I really enjoy it because its made make aa a bit, it pushing me to always come to class	
135	I	aha	
136	R	always come to class, did any assignment	
137	I	mm	
138	R	that she gave.	
139	I	So that's a new feeling.	
140	R	[ya]	
141	I	[How] about before this?	
142	R	Before this?	
143	I	aha	
144	R	{Laugh} I don't know, bef aaa like the short semester, aaa my teacher is not like aa my teacher aaa now	
145	I	aha	

146	R	aa he, eh, she a bit more quite something but	
147	I	mm	
148	R	when I … because what is make me bit disappointed is when in short semester, I think I write ok aa I come to aaaa the lecture, see discussion a bit discussion just aa aa scratch every thing, this is your problem, this is your problem and that's enough. Ok it's not really big problem because when I see ok it's not really big because the he didn't do anything with my [writing]	
149	I	[ok]	
150	R	but but unfortunately maybe, I failed again	
151	I	hmm	
152	R	I don't know why. Maybe aa sometimes with the absence, attendance because in the short semester I have to admit that that I have some problems with absence. And I I want to change it now. Ok maybe not only from the teacher but we have to introspect ourselves right? Maybe because the short semester make me a bit lazy I don't know.	
153	I	Hmm so was there ever one time that you thought that aaa writing or learning writing is difficult?	
154	R	Aaa I think it is not really difficult because what I like is aaa to how ok to study aa study aa writing is, I like to practice, practice a lot.	
155	I	hmm	
156	R	I like to practice because this is what I [need]	
157	I	[hmm]	

158	R	practice and see which one is my problem because even my teacher, said that you not really have a big problem maybe some grammar's here and your aa sentences, the xx (word unclear) coordination xx (word unclear) [maybe]	
159	I	[hmm]	
160	R	something problem with that.	
161	I	So so that's what your teacher said about [you]	
162	R	ahm	
163	I	so so you individually or personally	
164	R	[aha]	
165	I	[ya] aa, what what what are your, you know when you look into yourself personally, aaa which area do you think you are weak at, especially [in writing?]	RQ 2
166	R	[grammar] mostly grammar	
167	I	Grammar?	
168	R	Ya. Because sometimes I am confused but aa the grammar and aaa I mean xx (unclear word) for writing it's to find the idea	
169	I	aha	
170	R	aa sometimes. Maybe aa my teacher said that you have to read a read a lot read a lot, ya maybe I am not read a lot nowadays	
171	I	hmm	
172	R	because aa but I can read a lot, but aa sometimes the topics aa very I think about the [topic]	
173	I	[hmm]	

174	R	but I use, I will use lo.. aa logic, my logic to aaa to write and aa write my argument or something. Aaa maybe grammar and how to find the idea and vocabulary sometimes, that's my problem	
175	I	Ok right, so you that these are your weaknesses, [right]	
176	R	[ya]	
177	I	so I wonder if aa aa what what have you done to improve yourself in this area?	
178	R	Ok	
179	I	a'ha	
180	R	[For grammar]	
181	I	[honestly] honestly what you have done or whatbyou know have you [done anything?]	
182	R	[just] I think {laugh} I did very little thing I don't know	
183	I	mm	
184	R	for vocabulary I I start a little right now and find maybe some aa hard vocabularies like aa because alhamdullillah kulliyyah of economics allowed me even I am still in aaa celpad	
185	I	mm	
186	R	they allowed me I took three subjects	
187	I	mm	
188	R	aa I am taking three subjects now ...	
189	I	Are you a bridging student?	
190	R	No	
191	I	no	
192	R	I am not a bridging students. Aaa they said ok, you you can take aa from from these subject I learn many new vocabularies	
193	I	mm	

194	R	because I have to read a lot right? I just have to study or something also in management, accountancy, is they play a bit hard vocabulary rarely to see aa, this make me aa make me practice and practice and o I know and because sometimes I will bring my dictionaries	
195	I	mm	
196	R	to see what's the meaning, ooo this is ok, this is this is the meaning of this, this is the meaning of this, that so. For grammar, aa honestly I didn't study a lot about grammar because I don't know, I feel very bored about grammar but I don't know when aa I write if my lecturer aaa give me an exercise I can do, I will do it aaa maybe a bit mistakes but when I have to apply it on my writing, that's the problem. Sometimes I am a bit confused (laugh)	
197	I	[ooh]	
198	R	[ok,] what is this? (laugh), what is this?...	
199	I	So so mainly because you are confused?	
200	R	Yeah, confused	
201	I	Mmm. Interesting, ok right so now you have your teacher teaching you ...	
202	R	aha	
203	I	that's from your teacher's perspective how to teach you, but you as a student, if I were to give a chance	
204	R	[aha]	
205	I	[to tell] me what would you aaa think aaa will be the best way for you to learn? ok what would be the best way? Now we put you in class, your teacher teaches you how many hours?	
206	R	[I like..]	

207	I	[do you have now?] aa per week?	
208	R	Per week?	
209	I	A'ah.	
210	R	Aaaa [for]	
211	I	[four ya aha?]	
212	R	for writing?	
213	I	Ya four hours? No? more?	
214	R	More	
215	I	Ok, your contact hours? Do how how many times do you see your teacher	
216	R	[oook?]	
217	I	[per week]	
218	R	per weeks maybe about four hours …	
219	I	Four hours [ok]	
230	R	[Ya four hours]	
231	I	So that's our you know we thought that we should teach …	
232	R	ya	
233	I	…you but based on your perception, [your own …]	
234	R	[I think that's enough], I like because	
235	I	Aha mm	
236	R	like	
237	I	mm	
238	R	like my my teacher now, because sometimes teacher after aa they gave you an exercise	
239	I	mm	
240	R	ok, you write this, at least you write first is thesis statement first, co … and then come to see me, but mmm my teacher now is not like that	
241	I	mm	
242	R	she will walk around the class	
243	I	ahm	

244	R	see and make sure that every students doing anythings right. That's what I like, [and]	
245	I	[hmm]	
246	R	at least the teacher gi … gives gives some attention to the students so, ok, let me see – this is wrong, wrong, wrong, I better like even she have to aaa I don't know just crossing my or write anything in my paper	
247	I	Mm	
248	R	it's more better because I know that aaa, there is something wrong with my aaa writing and she will help me aaa to make it right.	
249	I	Ahmm	
250	R	That's what I like. Actually I like xx because now aa this about ok, aaa she always aaa what I like here is she, she is like but aaa it's like she is on fire to teach every students. [Because ….]	
251	I	[Every student], you mean … meaning she she pays attention to	
252	R	Yes yes	
253	I	[to everybody]	
254	R	she comes …] Ya ok maybe but aaa maybe sometimes she is a bit confused because there are so many students in the class [right]	
255	I	[definitely]	
256	R	ya. But at least she came every desk	
257	I	awh	
258	R	aaa see ok, this is wrong, this is wrong but may be it's not really aa aa don't have enough time aaa	
259	I	hmm	

260	R	but she tried to make it and I always asked about my writings, ooo you have mistakes in [here here here ...]	
261	I	So so] you believe that's how you learn best ya?	
262	R	Aaa ya	
263	I	aa	
264	R	insyaallah	
263	I	Aaa ok, aaa right, so aaa just now I was talking about, I asked you about wh.. in what area are you weak in ya so that it is in terms of the writing itself..	
264	R	hmm	
265	I	But now I want to focus on your learning, you know, your learning aa process. Ya, so aa as a student ya aaa what what difficulties do you face ya in order to learn writing itself? No, it's like maybe not the classroom, but aa perhaps aaa you learn you use books, resources, classrooms and so on ... ya because this will help you in learning. So, what are your difficulties, do you have any difficulties?	
266	R	When aa [studying	
267	I	Ya in] learning	
268	R	In learning?	
269	I	not in writing but in learning how to write?	
270	R	In learning how to write?	
271	I	Aha.. do you have any difficulties, it can be external, you know around you ...	
272	R	Hmm?	
273	I	books, resources, aaa opportunities to use the aaa to use writing	
274	R	[ya]	
275	I	[do you] have any problems?	

276	R	Because sometimes …	
277	I	ok what what are your problems?	
278	R	Aa but aa actually, on learning how to write	
279	I	ahm	
280	R	I don't really have much problem	
281	I	ok	
282	R	because fe now I am taking 3 subjects	
283	I	ahmm	
284	R	What I learning on the writing class, I can applied it to straightly to to my aa assignment. Ok.	
285	I	Ok.	
286	R	and I don't know, my teacher eh my lecturer aaa after I gave him an assignment, (laugh) he never gave back..	
287	I	[allright]	
288	R	..[never] gave back, I don't know which one is my mistake something but I don't have very much problem with that.	
289	I	So, so, so u think it helps you in fact?..	
290	R	[ya]	
291	I	…[for your] work in the kulliyyah	
292	R	ya	
293	I	But do you think your work in the kulliyyah affect the way aaa you learn in your writing class? Is there any effect?	
294	R	No	
295	I	No, ya?	
296	R	No	
297	I	No effect whatsoever ya? Hmmm ya because sa now you are doing you know like you are here, and you are one foot here, one foot there..	
298	R	[yeah] …	

299	I	So] I wonder if it affects you..	
300	R	ya	
300	I	so no ya?	
301	R	No no	
302	I	Ok. ok so aa my last few questions ya?aaa now aaa like aaa mmm since you say that you didn't have aa any proper problem at all, so I would say that as a person ya, ok, just now you talked about how do you learn best, but now probably, if I ask you to represent ya students in general, right, so aaa do you have any other suggestions on how aa can we, ya the teachers..	
303	R	ahmm	
304	I	…and celpad make aaa writing or learning writing more beneficial and successful for students?	
305	R	Ok	
306	I	aha	
307	R	what I see from my friends …	
308	I	Ok	
309	R	I don't know sometimes, may be they boring …	
310	I	Hmm	
311	R	right? Maybe you have to aaa maybe you can see that aaa many of students didn't came to class …	
312	I	ok	
313	R	..they prefer to sleep in their mahallah or something..	
314	I	hmm	
315	R	I don't know maybe aaa I think the the the teacher itself have to some kind of ability to make the class interesting.	
316	I	alright	

317	R	that's the first thing. Ok and the teacher also I think, owhh, make the class interesting first because it will aa attract them to come to the class, because but I think for that it is inside aa the students itself,	
318	I	ahm	
319	R	if they want to improve, I think it's no matter the teacher or something, if they want to improve, themselves, they they can improve themselves aaa by doing on their own. I think but for to improve on learning in celpad, actually celpad provide aa a good environment, aaa with aaa for lil for listening, for reading, everything, right, aaa for wri even for writing many topics many topics new topics always come with the new topics and I think aaa it's about to how to interact with the students not only me maybe I don I don't know. Aaa if aaa because you asked me to represent	
320	I	ya	
321	R	representing students right?	
322	I	ya	
323	R	aaa I think ya, that's the first thing. How to make the students in aa [inte …]	
324	I	Successful]	
325	I	You know so that the learning in of writing itself …	
326	R	ya	
327	I	…become [more successful]	
328	R	[Aha ya] Actually mostly on writing …	
329	I	ahah	

330	R	Because aa on class writing they I think, if I asked to my aaa friends that still studying in celpad they will a bit itst aaa, xx (word unclear) boring boring..	
331	I	hmm	
332	R	..boring boring, but if they have to listening or..	
333	I	mm	
334	R	..speaking maybe they a bit enjoy it right?	
335	I	A'ah	
336	R	Maybe for writing is aaa a bit change of the way aa how to ss how to educate the students, how to give them aa learning, aaa how to write, maybe, like aaa istct I think my teacher now, on aa on this semester is good actually. Aaa because aaa bec because aaa I really enjoy with her because he very good and handle everything nicely.	
336	I	You mean …	
338	R	[aa]	
339	I	…[handle] everything nicely means?	
340	R	that aaa to, aa you know, aaa the she not no in in the class aaa aaa in the sosdell lab 5 …	
341	I	alright	
342	R	…my classes, there is a many computer or something, she didn't aa apa, tidak melarang tidak melarang, she didn't aaa tidak melarang students mm aaa for aaa play with the internet …	
343	I	mm	
344	R	It's up to you …	
345	I	mm	

346	R	but maybe some websites is not maybe facebook nowadays or chatting or something, aaa most of the students did that and they will not concentrate on their writing ok.	
347	I	hmm	
348	R	…maybe its aaa haa handle is she handle the students alright ha very good. Because the students is not really play around, or something. Maybe some students a bit more lazy or something and they didn't finish his writing, it depends on on the student itself, right? But aaaa in my class, there is no talking each other …	
349	I	mm	
350	R	…make noisy …	
351	I	mm	
352	R	…or something, no, everybody writing, if aaa they bit boring about their writing, they open internet for a second …	
353	I	mm	
354	R	…then continue again …	
355	I	ya	
356	R	but most of the students finish …	
357	I	hmm	
358	T	…their writing.	

359	I	So, so, you think that will lead to successful and beneficial learning?	
360	R	Ya, beneficial learning.	
361	I	Ok	
362	R	Ok, so I have finished all my questions ...	
363	I	ya	
364	R	... I would like to thank you for your input and again I would like to say thank you again.	
END			

Appendix 3

A Sample Template In Generating Main Ideas for Four Research Questions (Rosnani Kassim 2016)

Research Question 1: How do poor L2 learners perceive learning to write in English?

Coding Template

Interview Question	Super ordinate	Subordinate	Elaboration	Occurrence	Frequency of Occurences	Ordering of Discourse Unit
		Main points form conversation not a summary	Examples from verbal to support the subordinate	Main idea transferred as key word(s) based on the summary of the subordinate fact(s)	Frequency of Main Idea – one main idea as one frequency	
	Key words of the questions					
	(2)		(4)			
		(3)		(5)		
					(6)	(7)
(1)						

Informant 1

Tell me something about your history of learning writing in English – when, how long?	History of learning	… I start learning English from the elementary school. So until now it's about aaa 13 years studying [English …	I am not aaa intentionally aaa study aa in how to write but because I always have problems with grammar …	13 years Basic English only Not writing per se		28–30
			…before I came here aaa I mm study in aa some of called the …	3 months EAP course (short course) in Indonesia		32
			…It's a like aaa international language programme … I studied there for academic, English for academic purposes …			38 40
			… it's not really long. Just for three months … …after my schooling years …			42 46
			I attend this university in north Sumatra medan before I came here … Short course …			48 50

How does your writing experience in school differ from your writing experience now?	Writing experience then and now	not really not intentionally	They just aaa like give me the if I study this grammar is like may be past participle …	In school, learned grammar and structure only		58–62
			some kind of it and they give me an example first aa the teacher explained …	Simple grammar exercises		64
			…something aa and she just gave me aa an exercise [that's all …]	Drilling		66
			we never learn how to write like maybe compare and contrast, argumentative essay or [something …]	Wasn't exposed to different modes of essays		68
			or to analyse pie charts …	Or analyzing data		70

			write write write because before, I in short the sh.. in the the last short semester	Essay writing		92
			the teacher onl.. aa sometimes explaining about the grammar grammar grammar {laugh} aa aa honestly I bored with [that]	Previous lecturer in university, some also taught grammar but grammar boring.		98
1. How do you feel about learning writing in English?	Feelings towards learning writing	[Ya sometimes] maybe aa sometimes maybe will be bored		Writing sometimes boring.	1	128

		Because aa on class writing they I think, if I asked to my aaa friends that still studying in celpad they will a bit itst aaa, xx (word unclear) boring..		Boring, just like how friends feel.	1	330

Research Question 3: What are the problems and challenges faced by the poor learners in learning writing?

Informant 1: Student 2

Interview Question	Super ordinate Key words of the questions	Subordinate Main points form conversation not a summary	Elaboration Examples from verbal to support the subordinate	Occurrence Main idea transferred as key word(s) based on the summary of the subordinate fact(s) (5)	Frequency Of Occurence Frequency of Main Idea- One Main idea as one frequency	Ordering of Discourse Unit
		(3)				
	(2)		(4)			(7)
(1)					(6)	

What are the difficulties that you face in learning writing?	Difficulties in learning writing.	I don't really have much problem	because fe now I am taking 3 subjects	**Not much problem.**		280-282
			What I learning on the writing class, I can applied it to straightly to my aa assignment	What learned in writing class useful for core courses' assignments		284
		I don't know, my teacher eh my lecturer aaa after I gave him an 7assignment, (laugh) he never gave back..	...gave back, I don't know which one is my mistake something but I don't have very much problem with that	Doesn't know own weaknesses Previous teacher didn't return assignment, student didn't know what to improve		286-288
		I don't know sometimes, may be they boring ...	Maybe you have to aaa maybe you can see that aaa many of students didn't came to class ...	Not interested to go to class.		309-311

			..they prefer to sleep in their mahallah or something..		313
In your opinion, what are the factors that are causing the difficulties you mentioned before?	Causes for difficulties.	I don't know, my teacher eh my lecturer aaa after I gave him an 7assignment, (laugh) he never gave back..	...gave back, I don't know which one is my mistake something but I don't have very much problem with that	The teacher wasn't helpful	286-288

Research Question 4: How do the students overcome the challenges they face in L2 writing?

Informant 1:   Student 2

Interview Question	Super ordinate	Subordinate	Elaboration	Occurrence	Frequency Of Occurence	Ordering of Discourse Unit
		Main points form conversation not a summary	Examples from verbal to support the subordinate	Main idea transferred as key word(s) based on the summary of the subordinate fact(s)	Frequency of Main Idea- One Main idea as one frequency	
			(4)	(5)		
		(3)				
(1)	(2)				(6)	
						(7)
What do you do to overcome the problems?	Steps to overcome challenges.	None.				

Are they effective?		None.				
What would you suggest to make learning writing more successful and beneficial for students?		I don't know maybe aaa I think the the the teacher itself have to some kind of ability to make the class interesting	make the class interesting first because it will aa attract them to come to the class	Teacher makes class more interesting.		315-317
		...if they want to improve, themselves, they they can improve themselves aaa by doing on their own		Students should study on their own		319

		but for to improve on learning in celpad, actually celpad provide aa a good environment	for listening, for reading, everything, right, aaa for wri even for writing many topics many topics new topics always come with the new topics	xxxxxprovides good environment for language learning		319
		I think aaa it's about to how to interact with the students not only me maybe I don I don't know		Teacher should know how to interact with students		319

		Maybe for writing is aaa a bit change of the way aa how to ss how to educate the students, how to give them aa learning, aaa how to write,		Teacher should teach students how to write		336
			…my classes, there is a many computer or something, she didn't aa apa, tidak melarang tidak melarang, she didn't aaa tidak melarang students mm aaa for aaa play with the internet …	Allows use the internet in class while doing writing.	1	342
			…or something, no, everybody writing, if aaa they bit boring about their writing, they open internet for a second …	Allows use internet if students want a break.	1	352
			It's up to you …	Gives freedom to relax – not too strict.		344

			..but maybe some websites is not maybe facebook nowadays or chatting or something, aaa most of the students did that and they will not concentrate on their writing ok.	Always reminds to use it in the right ways.		346
		...maybe its aaa haa handle is she handle the students alright ha very good.	Because the students is not really play around, or something. Maybe some students a bit more lazy or something and they didn't finish his writing, it depends on on the student itself, right? But aaaa in my class, there is no talking each other ...	Teachers should know how to handle students. Stresses on discipline too. Asserting control.	1	348–348

Appendix 4a

A Sample Template in Generating Themes

Research Question 1: How do poor L2 learners perceive learning to write in English?

Interview Questions	Main ideas	Subthemes	Themes
1. Tell me something about your history of learning writing in English – when, how long?	1. 13 years (R2) 2. Basic English only (R2) 3. Not writing per say (R2) 4. 3 months EAP course (short course) in Indonesia (R2) 5. Didn't learn writing at all (R1) 6. Just learned grammar and speaking (R1) 7. For grammar, drilling practice (R1) 8. Learned at high school (R1) 9. Mostly grammar exercises multiple choice (R1) 10. Also write sentence level (R1)		School College

2.	How does your writing experience in school differ from your writing experience now?	1.	In school- learned grammar and structure only (R2)	Grammar lessons	School
		2.	Simple grammar exercises (R2)		
		3.	Drilling (R2)		
		4.	Wasn't exposed to different modes of essays (R2)	Grammar and sentence	
		5.	Or analyzing data (R2)	structure	
		6.	Essay writing (R2)	learned	
		7.	Previous lecturer in university, some also taught grammar but grammar boring (R2)	through drilling.	University
		8.	In Indonesia sentences only (R1)	No exposure	
		9.	Now in UIA, write essays (R1)	to essay	
		10.	Sentences written on grammar items (R1)	writing	
				Essay	

3.	How do you feel about learning writing in English?	1.	Writing sometimes boring (R2)		
		2.	Boring, just like how friends feel (R2)	Boring	
		3.	Enjoy because likes the way lecturer teaches (R2)		
		4.	Motivated (R2)		Negative feelings
				Enjoyable	
		5.	Doesn't like the way previous teacher taught (R2)		
		6.	Short semester- disappointed (R2)	Motivated	
		7.	Teacher didn't explain weaknesses (R2)		
		8.	Didn't feel like going to class,- lazy (R2)	Dissatisfied Lazy	Positive feelings
		9.	Writing not really difficult (R2)	Not difficult	
		10.	Likes to practice.Needs to practice a lot (R2)		
		11.	He feels good learning writing (R1)		
		12.	Generally feels good (R1)		
		13.	Feels happy (R1)		
		14.	Sometimes doesn't have the mood for it (R1)		
		15.	Feels bored (R1)		

Research Question 2: What Are The Needs Of The Students In L2 Writing?

Interview Questions	Main ideas	Subthemes	Themes
1. In your opinion, in what areas are you weak at in learning writing in English?	1. Mostly grammar (R2) 2. Confused with grammar (R2) 3. Weak at getting ideas (R2) 4. Weak at understanding the topic (R2) 5. Grammar, ideas and vocabulary (R2) 6. To apply what have been learned. Confused (R2) 7. Weak in vocabulary (R1) 8. Weak in writing correct and grammatical sentences -grammar (R1) 9. Sometimes difficult to get ideas for the topic (R1) 10. Getting the ideas (R1) 11. Brainstorming is difficult (R1) 12. Weak in vocabulary, grammar and ideas (R1) 13. Sometimes no problem with ideas but problem sentence structure and organization (R1)		Grammar Ideas Vocabulary Structure and organization

2.	What do you usually do to improve yourself in writing?	1.	The interviewee did not do much (R2)		
		2.	Review vocabulary from courses taken at kulliyyah (R2)		Nothing much
		3.	Try to improve vocabulary by reading and looking up words in dictionary (R2)	Read notes and coursebook	
		4.	Rarely study grammar. Bored with it (R2)	for core courses to	Reading
		5.	Reread own essays to look at the right way to write especially organization and grammar(R1)	improve vocabulary	
		6.	Reads samples given by lecturer to find meaning of difficult vocabulary (R1)	Read essays	
		7.	Read written work for core courses to look at the right way to write and learn vocabulary (R1)		

3.	How do you think you will learn best?	1.	4 hours enough. Not more (R2)		
		2.	Teacher checks on each student (R2)		
		3.	Makes sure students do the right thing (R2)	Not too long	
		4.	Individual attention is given to each student (R2)		
		5.	Teacher should explain to students clearly and honestly about their weaknesses (R2)	Individual attention	Class duration
		6.	Teacher explains students' weaknesses and helps to correct (R2)	Clear explanation	Teacher's disposition
		7.	Even though many students, teacher gives individual attention to each student (R2)	Student autonomy	Teaching approach
		8.	Explains to students clearly (R2)	Modelling	
		9.	Even not enough time, teacher will talk to each student (R2)		
		10.	Lecturer allows student to choose own topic to write (R1)		
		11.	Lecturer writes together with sudents in the class on the same topic. Then show to students and explain his essay (R1)		

Research Question 3: What Are The Problems And Challenges Faced By The Poor Learners In Learning Writing?

Interview Questions	Main ideas	Sub-themes	Themes
1. What are the difficulties that you face in learning writing?	1. Not much problem (R2) 2. What learned in writing class useful for core courses' assignments (R2) 3. Doesn't know own weaknesses. (R2) 4. Previous teacher didn't return assignment, student didn't know what to improve (R2) 5. Not interested to go to class. (R2) 6. No problems (R1) 7. All he needs are available (R1) 8. Resources easy to get (R1) 9. Classroom no problems (R1) 10. No difficulties but rather, laziness (R1) 11. Not in the mood (R1) 12. Sometimes bored (R1) 13. Motivation is a problem (R1) 14. Not understanding own weaknesses. Doesn't know why keeps on failing (R1)	No problem Lack of motivation Not knowing own weaknesses	External Internal

| 2. | In your opinion, what are the factors that are causing the difficulties you mentioned before? | 1. The teacher wasn't helpful (R2)
2. Having to repeat the same course (R1)
3. Having to learn the same thing over and over again (R1)
4. Repeating (R1)
5. Teacher doesn't explain weaknesses (R1) | | Teacher

Repeating the same course |

Research Question 4: How Do The Students Overcome The Challenges They Face In L2 Writing?

Interview Questions	Main ideas	Sub-themes	Themes
1. What do you do to overcome the problems in learning writing?	1. Focus in class (R1) 2. Think positively (R1) 3. Sometimes gives up (R1) 4. Try to forget writing and CELPAD by reading core courses' notes (R1) 5. Looks at writing samples (R1) 6. Read the samples (R1) 7. Less writing, more reading (R1)	Psychologically Revise by reading	Positive coping mechanism Negative coping mechanism
2. Are they effective?	1. Reading helps (R1)		Yes

3.	What would you suggest to make learning writing more successful and beneficial for students?	1.	Teacher makes class more interesting (R2)		
		2.	Students should study on their own (R2)	Interesting class	
		3.	CELPAD provides good environment for language learning (R2)		University
				Self study	
		4.	Teacher should know how to interact with students (R2)		
		5.	Teacher should teach students how to write (R2)		Teacher
		6.	Allows students to use the internet in class while doing writing. (R2)	Condusive environment	
		7.	Allows use internet if students want a break. (R2)	Understanding	
		8.	Gives freedom to relax – not too strict. (R2)		
		9.	Always reminds to use freedom in the right ways (R2)		Student
				Firm	
		10.	Stresses on discipline too. Asserting control (R2)		
		11.	Ensures students complete writing (R2)		
		12.	Teach what will be tested (R1)	Knows how to teach	
		13.	Same level as exam (R2)		
		14.	Teacher focuses on aspects tested (R2)	Focus on exam	

Appendix 4b

A Sample Template in Generating Themes (Hazlina Abdullah 2012)

Research Question 2:	What are the teachers' understandings of "motivation" in learning English as a second language?			
Interview Question 6:	What does "motivation" in the context of learning an L2 mean to you?			
Informant 1 (I1)	Informant 2 (I2)	Informant 3 (I3)	Subthemes	Themes
Short term goal – passing examinations Having choices	Interest to learn the language.	Internal factors. Regulate own learning strategies. External aspects complementing the internal aspects. Independent learning.		Intrinsic motivation Extrinsic motivation

Appendix 5

Summarised Themes Based on RQs and
IQs (Rosnani Kassim 2016)

Research Question 2: What are the needs of the students in L2 writing?

Interview Q	Themes	Sub themes	Main Ideas	R	DU	Transcriptions
In your opinion, in what areas are you weak at in learning writing in English?	Grammar		Mostly grammar	R2	166	[grammar] mostly grammar
			Confused with grammar	R2	168	Because sometimes I am confused but aa the grammar ...
			Weak in writing correct and grammatical sentences	R1	76	...kedua yang ke kedua yang kedua seperti apa a untuk menjadikan ayat tu lebih sempurna saya sempurna dalam grammar saya memang kurang masih kurang.
			Grammar, ideas and vocabulary	R2	174	but I use, I will use lo.. aa logic, my logic to aaa to write and aa write my argument or something. Aaa maybe grammar and how to find the idea and vocabulary sometimes, that's my problem

				R2	196	I don't know when aa I write if my lecturer aaa give me an exercise I can do, I will do it aaa maybe a bit mistakes but when I have to apply it on my writing, that's the problem. Sometimes I am a bit confused (laugh)
			To apply what have been learned. Confused			
Ideas			Getting the ideas	R1	86	...secara umum yang kita memang kita memang apa mengetahuinya secara secara tak tak tak tak tak semua orang tahu la.
			Weak at understanding topic	R2	172	sometimes the topics aa very I think about the [topic]
			Weak at getting ideas	R2	168	... for writing it's to find the idea
			Getting the ideas	R1	88	macam aa disease entah aa kesihatan itu aa kadang apa untuk mendapatkan idea itu payah madam.
			Brainstorming is difficult	R1	90	Aa brainstorming aa itu agak susah madam.
			Grammar, ideas and vocabulary	R2	174	but I use, I will use lo.. aa logic, my logic to aaa to write and aa write my argument or something. Aaa maybe grammar and how to find the idea and vocabulary sometimes, that's my problem
Vocabulary			Grammar ideas and vocabulary	R2	174	but I use, I will use lo.. aa logic, my logic to aaa to write and aa write my argument or something. Aaa maybe grammar and how to find the idea and vocabulary sometimes, that's my problem
			Weak in vocabulary	R1	74	Pertama saya mungkin kurang di vocabularies.
			Weak in vocabulary, grammar and ideas	R1	94	Ahm (vocabulary, grammar and ideas).

	Structure and organization			Sometimes no problem with ideas but problem with structure and organization	R1	298	Itulah aaa kadang madam kadang sebagian topic itu memang saya dapat idea tapi saya kurang bisa untuk atur idea itu semua bisa susun rapi saya memang kurang memang.
What do you usually do to improve yourself in writing?	Nothing much			The interviewee didn't do much to improve his writing	R2	182	[just] I think {laugh} I did very little thing I don't know
				Rarely study grammar. Bored with it	R2	196	to see what's the meaning, ooo this is ok, this is this is the meaning of this, this is the meaning of this, that so. For grammar, aa honestly I didn't study a lot about grammar because I don't know, I feel very bored about grammar
	Reading	Read notes and coursebook for core courses to improve vocabulary	Try to improve vocabulary by reading and looking up words in dictionary		R2	194	because I have to read a lot right? I just have to study or something also in management, accountancy, is they play a bit hard vocabulary rarely to see aa, this make me aa make me practice and practice and o I know and because sometimes I will bring my dictionaries
			Review vocabulary from courses taken at kulliyyah		R2	184 192	...alhamdullillah kulliyyah of economics allowed me even I am still in aaa celpad I am not a bridging students. Aaa they said ok, you you can take aa from from these subject I learn many new vocabularies
			Read written work for core courses to look at the right way to write and learn vocabulary		R1	118	Aa kadang-kadang dalam subjek kuliah itu saya medapatkan writing writing jugak. Kadang-kadang saya baca satu persatu tu saya fahami cara menulisnya dan vo.. apa vocab vocab yang ada dalam yang itunya.

			Read essays	Reread own essays to look at the right way to write especially organization and grammar	R1	98 -102	...saya aa setiap aa apa lecture bagi topic saya selalu refer untuk ada saya punya writing, punya writing dari lecture saya aa apa saya selalu refer ke ini ke ke topic itu walaupun topiknya berbeda tapi secara formalnya saya mengi ... mengikuti stuk apa strukturnya situ. ... Cara cara menulis ayat ... ...Aaa (boleh bantu grammar).
				Read samples given by lecturer to find meaning of difficult vocabulary	R1	106 108	[Aa] biasanya itulah biasanya say aaa baca-baca sample sample dari writing yang dibagi oleh lecture. Yang saya tak tahu saya saya cari makna
How do you think you will learn best?	Class duration	Not too long	4 hours enough		R2	218 234	per weeks maybe about four hours ... [I think that's enough], I like because ...
	Teacher's dispositions	Individual attention	Teacher checks on each student		R2	240	ok, you write this, at least you write first is thesis statement first, co ... and then come to see me, but mmm my teacher now is not like that
			Individual attention is given to each student		R2	246	at least the teacher gi ... gives gives some attention to the students so, ok ...
			Makes sure students do the right thing		R2	244	see and make sure that every students doing anythings right. That's what I like, [and]

			Even though many students, teacher gives individual attention to each student	R2	254	she comes ...] Ya ok maybe but aaa maybe sometimes she is a bit confused because there are so many students in the class [right]
					256	ya. But at least she came every desk
			Even not enough time, teacher will talk to each student	R2	258	may be it's not really aa aa don't have enough time aaa ...
					260	...but she tried to make it and I always asked about my writings, ooo you have mistakes in [here here here ...]
		Clear explanation	Teacher should explain to students clearly and honestly about their weaknesses	R2	246	...let me see – this is wrong, wrong, wrong, I better like even she have to aaa I don't know just crossing my or write anything in my paper
			Teacher explains students' weaknesses and helps to correct	R2	248	it's more better because I know that aaa, there is something wrong with my aaa writing and she will help me aaa to make it right.
			Explain to students clearly	R2	258	this is wrong, this is wrong but may be it's not really aa aa don't have enough time aaa
	Teaching approach	Student autonomy	Lecturer allows him to choose own topic to write	R1	138	Apa kalau lecture tu boleh bagi apa? Aaa waktu apa lecture suruh pilih topic sendiri sama student sa aaaaa apa aa topiknya terserah pada student apa nak buat.
		Modelling	Lecturer writes together with sudents in the class on the same topic. Then show to students and explain his essay	R1	166	[Itulah] saya aaa harapan saya ada harapan nanti satu hari lecture bagi topic setelah suruh tulis sama kami
					170	lecture siap satu writing jugak. Nanti perlihatkan sama student perjelaskan ni cam ni cam ni. Aaa.(tajuk yang sama dengan pelajar).

Appendix 6

Inter-rater Reliability Form and Sample (Rosnani Kassim 2016)

SQ 1	Themes	Main ideas	Verbal support	Rater 1		Rater 2	
				Agree	Disagree	Agree	Disagree
IQ 2: What is writing to you? What is your perception towards writing?	Crucial	Writing is important	Informant 1 (I1)	first aa writing like the public card for me. Public transportation for me like public transportation because with the writing I can go to anywhere what I want.	Agree		Agree	
		Writing is important	Informant 3 (I3)	Ya my ticket to pass.	Agree		Agree	
	Insignificant	English/ writing is secondary.	Informant 3 (I3)	.. aa so it make me it's ok I have another subject so English is second one so it's ok.	Agree		Agree	

		Just for passing Little use for future	Informant 5 (I5)	I think aa it's just aa for passing the the EPT. For my future I'm not sure it's very useful or not useful..	Agree		Agree	
	Difficult	Difficult	Informant 4 (I4)	Difficult	Agree		Agree	

	Themes	Main ideas	Verbal support	Rater 1		Rater 2	
				Agree	Disagree	Agree	Disagree
IQ 3: How did you feel when you failed again?	Miserable	Very sad	Informant 2 (I2)	Mm, every time finish my exam.. ..I will call my mother … and my mother will ask me results, I am so sad about that.	Agree		Agree	
		Severely depressed	Informant 3 (I3)	.. at this time I get depression. Um I just you know everything be dark I don't know because you know I start quizzes {in bridging classes} and aa I see um be aa active in my [classes]..	Agree		Agree	

| | | Despair | Informant 4 (I4) | But when in the 4th semester, I feel that aa like I can't do it. I think I can cannot do everything because it's still in here. | Agree | | Agree | |
| | | Very sad | Informant 5 (I5) | (Sigh) I (pause) very sad I think.{When I failed again}. I because I I think I already pay all my energy on the exam. EPT exam but I ... continue fail. . so I very sad. | Agree | | Agree | |

| Positive | More motivated to study and pass | Informant 1 (I1) | Aa I have more spirits to catch the good band get aa the the maybe only in aa until the requirement aa to study to kulliyyah and for EPT I I feel optimist to exit this semester | Agree | | Agree | |
| | Optimistic | Informant 4 (I4) | Aa when to go to to 2 semesters to 2nd semester in in English, aa I think aa aa it is ok, I just do my little more aa effort to exit. | Agree | | Agree | |

SQ4	Themes	Subthemes	Main ideas	Verbal support		Rater 1		Rater 2	
						Agree	Disagree	Agree	Disagree
IQ 1: How do you think you will learn best?	Teacher	Teacher's guidance	Guidance by teacher	Infor mant 1 (I1)	Aa the teacher tell me step by step what's my problem. This your problem you can do it like this, if you not understand you can the other way to make the best sentence what you can do, what you can said to with another.	Agree		Agree	

			Teacher explains errors and helps make corrections.	Informant 2 (I2)	[I think] aa if teacher have free time.... mm I I can take my essay to.... her and aa.. .. mm where is wrong and she tell tell me.... or this sentence.... mm how to write is correct.... or how to write real good....I think I like this.	Agree		Agree	
		Teacher's disposition	Helpful teacher	Informant 3 (I3)	Ya ... helpful teacher. ..um she show us this is the mistake you have to write something here ...	Agree		Agree	
			Patient teacher	Informant 3 (I3)	[And.. and] ya and patient teacher.	Agree		Agree	

		Activities suitable for individual student	Infor mant 2 (I2)	Mm, teacher mm this teacher just give us some paper about wrong sentence.. paragraph. (Laughs), because I don't like so, I think. Maybe mm it good for others students but for me, I think aa (laughs) cannot. Mm because aa mm I don't like aa correct the sentence (laughs).	Agree		Agree	Disagree (provide acts which cater to stds' language needs)
Extra practice		Teachers hould give more homework	Infor mant 1 (I1)	Also give homework.. Both. {doing in-class work and homework both helped me}.	Agree		Agree	
		More exercises	Infor mant 2 (I2)	Mm, I think I thought ok but aa need give us more exercise..	Agree		Agree	
		Do exercises on reading and grammar	Infor mant 3 (I3)	Exercise. Um reading ..... exercise, grammar..	Agree		Agree	
		Write more	Infor mant 4 (I4)	I wish aa she want extra exercise to.. ... correct it. Yes. {I am willing to write extra}.	Agree			Disagree (Stds wish to write more)

Inter-Rater Reliability Form (Sample)

Understanding Repeating-Repeaters in an ESL Writing Course: A Case Study of Pre-Sessional Students in IIUM (Rosnani Kassim 2016)

Themes	Main ideas	Verbal support		Rater 1		Rater 2	
				Agree	Disagree	Agree	Disagree
IQ 3: How did you feel when you failed again?	Miserable	Very sad	Informant 2 (I2)	Mm, every time finish my exam.. ..I will call my mother.. ..and my mother will ask me results, I am so sad about that.	Agree		Agree	
		Severely depressed	Informant 3 (I3)	.. at this time I get depression. Um I just you know everything be dark I don't know because you know I start quizzes {in bridging classes} and aa I see um be aa active in my [classes]..	Agree		Agree	
		Despair	Informant 4 (I4)	But when in the 4th semester, I feel that aa like I can't do it. I think I can cannot do everything because it's still in here.	Agree		Agree	
		Very sad	Informant 5 (I5)	(Sigh) I (pause) very sad I think.{When I failed again}. I because I I think I already pay all my energy on the exam. EPT exam but I.. .. continue fail. . ..so I very sad.	Agree		Agree	

					Rater 1		Rater 2	
Positive	More motivated to study and pass.	Infor mant 1 (I1)	Aa I have more spirits to catch the good band get aa the the maybe only in aa until the requirement aa to study to kulliyyah and for EPT I I feel optimist to exit this semester		Agree		Agree	
	Optimistic	Infor mant 4 (I4)	Aa when to go to to 2 semesters to 2nd semester in in English, aa I think aa aa it is ok, I just do my little more aa effort to exit.		Agree		Agree	

SQ4	Themes	Subthemes	Main ideas	Verbal support	Rater 1		Rater 2	
					Agree	Disagree	Agree	Disagree
IQ 1: How do you think you will learn best?	Teacher	Teacher's guidance	Guidance by teacher.	Infor mant 1 (I1)	Aa the teacher tell me step by step what's my problem. This your problem you can do it like this, if you not understand you can the other way to make the best sentence what you can do, what you can said to with another.	Agree		Agree	
			Teacher explains errors and helps make correc tions.	Infor mant 2 (I2)	[I think] aa if teacher have free time.... mm I I can take my essay to.... her and aa.. .. mm where is wrong and she tell tell me.... or this sentence.... mm how to write is correct....or how to write real good....I think I like this.	Agree		Agree	
		Teacher's disposition	Helpful teacher	Infor mant 3 (I3)	Ya ... helpful teacher. ..um she show us this is the mistake you have to write something here ...	Agree		Agree	

			Patient teacher	Infor mant 3 (I3)	[And.. and] ya and patient teacher.	Agree		Agree	
			Approa chable teacher	Infor mant 5 (I5)	I think Zubaidah teacher is better..[Because because you] know aa her [character].... you know, lovely so aa [we we feel we feel].... we feel um aa not nervous. We feel relax.	Agree		Agree	
Various acti vities			Teacher to do new activities in class	Infor mant 1 (I1)	Like the ff ya new thing from the teacher, from my friends from the the planning study in the class, how to teacher the manage the class. You know the last semester almost discuss in the class. Discuss and discuss, so, discuss this the exercise my speaking..	Agree		Agree	
			Encourage students to identify and correct own errors	Infor mant 1 (I1)	And this semester I feel is focus to writing more writing. Do it the writing, check the writing, check the sent.. together. If it check it together I get new words from the other friend, I check, owh this my problem owh, is can do it. Always what the teacher said, do in in the class, I do it again in my room.	Agree		Agree	

121

			Activities suitable for individual student	Infor mant 2 (I2)	Mm, teacher mm this teacher just give us some paper about wrong sentence.. paragraph. (Laughs), because I don't like so, I think. Maybe mm it good for others students but for me, I think aa (laughs) cannot. Mm because aa mm I don't like aa correct the sentence (laughs).	Agree		Agree	Disagree (provide acts which cater to stds' language needs)
	Extra practice		Teacher should give more home work.	Infor mant 1 (I1)	Also give homework.. Both. {doing in-class work and homework both helped me}.	Agree		Agree	
			More exercises	Infor mant 2 (I2)	Mm, I think I thought ok but aa need give us more exercise..	Agree		Agree	
			Do exercises on reading and grammar.	Infor mant 3 (I3)	Exercise. Um reading..... exercise, grammar..	Agree		Agree	
			Write more	Infor mant 4 (I4)	I wish aa she want extra exercise to...., correct it. Yes. {I am willing to write extra}.	Agree			Disagree (Stds wish to write more)

Overall comments:

_____

_____

_____

_____

_____

_____

_____

Name: _____

Signature: _____ Date: _____

Designation: _____

Appendix 7

A Sample of an Audit Trail (Rosnani Kassim 2016)

Audit Trail

Preparing for fieldwork		
Date	**Activities**	**Records/ Sources**
19 Sept 2012	Received a letter to carry out research from INSTED.	Approval letter
19 Sept 2012	Met the Dean of CELPAD. Obtained approval to carry out research in CELPAD.	Verbal approval
19 Sept 2012	Contacted the coordinator of level 6 and requested for the names of the instructors teaching level 6.	Telephone call
19–20 Sept 2012	Emailed the instructors and all the instructors replied by stating that they were willing to help in identifying the students who fit the criteria determined by the researcher.	Email, telephone calls and selection criteria
26 Sept 2012	Instructors provided the researcher with the names and contact numbers of the students	Telephone calls

27 Sept 2012	20 students were identified by the instructors and all were approached by the researcher through the phone but only eight were willing to participate.	Telephone calls
28 Sept 2012	Prepared the note books for students to write their diary entries. Instructions and format adapted from literature.	Alaszewski, A. (2006). Nicholl, H. (2010).
1 Oct 2012	Met students to explain to them about the research.	Info on research topic, purpose and research questions.
2 Oct 2012	Set a meeting with the five students who were selected.	Telephone calls
3 Oct 2012	During the second meeting, the researcher distributed a form to all the five students to seek their written consent to participate in the study (Appendix 1). It was during this meeting also that the researcher gave the students RM30.00 each for their phone bills so that the students could contact the researcher through phone calls or short messaging system (SMS) anytime without worrying about the cost. Students signed the consent form. The researcher gave them the diary. The researcher enquired from the five students who their instructors in the previous and current semester were.	Consent form and empty diary.

4 Oct 2012	Contacted instructors through email. In the email, the researcher expressed her intention and provided the instructors with some background of the study with its aims. The researcher also sought the instructors' permission to interview them and all of them replied through email/phone that they agreed to meet the researcher.	Email and telephone calls
5 Oct 2012	The researcher contacted and met each instructor separately and during the meeting the instructors gave their verbal agreement to be interviewed and the interview dates were determined. The researcher planned a two-phase interview sessions. Phase 1: During the semester for the students' ex writing teachers. Phase 2: After the semester ended for the students' current writing teachers.	Verbal agreement

Fieldwork		
Date	**Activities**	**Records/ sources**
3 Oct 2012	Students began diary writing	Field note
12 Oct 2012	Checked student diary entries – Mas.	Students' diaries
16 Oct 2012	Interviewed Mr Shahbuddeen (Ex-teacher) Interviewed Ms Fateeya (Ex-teacher)	Interview guide, recorded interviews and transcribed interviews

| 16 Oct 2012 | Checked student diary entries – Cahaya, Zain, and Aisyah
Field observation note(on diary entries):
General: Students tend to summarize their writing lessons for example what they learned that day.
Specific:
Zain – wrote about his writing experience but too general so the researcher asked him to share specific events that would highlight his feelings and problems. He explained that it was his first time writing a diary, so he did not really know how to do it. So the researcher said just try to follow her advice and he will get used to it over the time.
Aisyah – very good. Very expressive. She wrote her feelings clearly but not much was written about her problems. So the researcher told her to also record her problems in learning writing in class.
Cahaya – her entries were mostly on learning English in general but not on writing. So the researcher asked her to focus on learning writing.
Field observation note (while having a casual chat with students):
Aisyah and Zain said they were confident when they write but they were always surprised when they got back their essay only to find out they failed. This made them feel frustrated. | Students' diaries and field notes |

17 Oct 2012	Checked student diary entries – Nur Field observation note (on diary entries): Entries were too general. So the researcher asked her to follow the samples and focus on specific events that can highlight her feelings and problems. Field observation note (while having a casual chat with students): Nur clearly had a study skill problem. For instance, she asked the researcher how to find books for writing practice. The researcher showed her some books but she said she did not know how to use the books and couldn't find what she needed. So the researcher taught her how to use the books. She said nobody had ever taught her how to use the reference and exercise books in the resource centre. Very surprising that she said she had never been to the library and did not even know how to use the online catalogue to find books.	Students' diaries and field notes
18 Oct 2012	Interviewed Mdm Khadija (Ex-teacher) Interviewed Mr Khalid (Ex-teacher) Interviewed Ms Rosmah (Ex-teacher) **Instructors signed consent form	Interview guide, recorded interviews, transcribed interviews and consent form
30 Oct 2012	Checked student diary entries.	Students' diaries
16 Nov	Checked student diary entries. During the session, the researcher set the dates to interview the students individually.	Students' diaries

20 Nov 2012	Received an SMS from Zain. Field observation note: He sounded panicked and desperate . It read "Madam A said with I did not progress with writing my essay Task 1. This make me confused and afraid. I think I do maximum exercise madam. She said about SVA (subject verb agreement)."	Field note
29 Nov 2012	Interview session with Mas and Aisyah (individually).	Interview guide, recorded interviews and transcribed interviews
3 Dec 2012	Interview session with Cahaya and Nur (individually).	Interview guide, recorded interviews and transcribed interviews
5 Dec 2012	Interview session with Zain. After the interview, the researcher enquired about the text message that he sent on 20 Nov 2012. Field observation note: The researcher asked him about it and he said at that time he was surprised and afraid. He panicked hearing the comment from his writing instructor because the mid-term exam was near but he was not making progress. He talked to his teacher later and he felt better. According to him "I saw the light".	Interview guide, recorded interviews, transcribed interviews and field notes

5 – 7 Dec 2012	Checked student diary entries. Since the students would sit for their IGA (in-class graded assessment) and the English Placement Test soon, the researcher asked them to write their feelings, attitudes and reflections in their entries on the upcoming exams.	Students' diaries
5 Dec 2012	Met Nur and Aisyah (together) to check their diaries.	Students' diaries
7 Dec 2012	Met Cahaya individually to review her diary. Field observation note: Cahaya confessed to the researcher that she had problem managing her time during exam. She also complained about not being able to think of supporting ideas.	Students' diaries and field notes
7 Dec 2012	Met Mas individually to review her diary. Field observation note: Mas believed that she was not treated fairly by her teacher because she felt the teacher did not like her. Also, when she approached her teacher she wanted her teacher to spoon-feed her and tell her her problems but she was not happy because her teacher asked her to identify her own problems instead.	Students' diaries and field notes
18/19 Dec 2012	Students returned diaries.	Students' diaries
21 Dec 2012	Last day of class for students.	

3 – Jan 2012	Interview with current instructors – Mdm Isma, Mr Khalid and Mdm Khadija (individually). **Instructor signed consent form (Mdm Rita and Mdm Isma)	Interview guide, recorded interviews, transcribed interviews and consent form
22 Feb 2013	Members checking	Transcribed interviews
22 Feb 2013	Post interview with Zain – scheduled after the researcher reviewed his transcribed interview and found that he did not really provide answers for some of the research questions.	Interview guide, recorded interviews and transcribed interviews

Bibliography

Allen, Charlotte. "Spies like Us: When Sociologists Deceive Their Subjects". *Lingua Franca* (November 1997): 31–38. http://linguafranca.mirror.theinfo.org/9711/9711.allen.html.

Baez, Benjamin. "Confidentiality in Qualitative Research: Reflections on Secrets, Power and Agency". *Qualitative Research* 2, no. 1 (April 2002): 35–58.

Bazeley, Pat. "Analysing Qualitative Data: More Than Identifying Themes". *Malaysian Journal of Qualitative Research* 2, no. 2, (2009): 6–22.

Birks, Melanie and Jane Mills. *Grounded Theory: A Practical Guide.* London: Sage Publications Ltd., 2011.

Bryman, Alan. *Social Research Methods.* Oxford: Oxford University Press, 2011.

Burgess, Robert. *In the Field: An Introduction to Field Research (Contemporary Social Research).* London: George Allen and Unwin, 1984.

Burnard, P., Gill, P., Stewart, K., Treasure, E., and B. Chadwick, B. "Analysing and Presenting Qualitative Data". *British Dental Journal* 204, no. 8 (26 April 2008): 429–32. doi:10.1038/sj.bdj.2008.292.

Cohen, Louis and Lawrence Manion and Keith Morrison. *Research Methods in Education.* New York: Routledge, 2011.

Creswell, John. *Planning, Conducting, and Evaluating Quantitative and Qualitative Research,* 4th ed. Boston: Pearson, 2012.

_____. *Qualitative Inquiry and Research Design: Choosing among Five Traditions.* Thousand Oaks, CA: Sage Publications, 1998.

Davidson, Christina. "Transcription: Imperatives for Qualitative Research". *International Journal of Qualitative Methods* 8 no. 2 (2009): 36–52.

Denzin, Norman and Yvonna Lincoln. *Handbook of Qualitative Research,* 2nd ed. Thousands Oak, CA: Sage Publications, March 18, 2000.

Glaser, Barney and Anselm Strauss. *The Discovery of Grounded Theory: Strategies for Qualitative Research.* New York: Aldine De Gruyter, 1967.

Grbich, Carol. *Qualitative Data Analysis: An Introduction.* London: Sage Publications, 2007.

Gumperz, John and Norine Berenz. "Transcribing Conversational Exchanges" (99–120). In *Talking Data: Transcription and Coding in Discourse Research.* Edwards, Jane and Martin Lampert, Eds. New York: Lawrence Erlbaum, 1993.

Hazlina Abdullah. *Attitudes and Motivation toward Learning the English Language among Students from an Islamic Education System Background: Exploring the Views of Teachers.* Unpublished manuscript, Kulliyyah of Education, International Islamic University, Malaysia, 2012.

Holloway, Immy. *Basic Concepts for Qualitative Research.* London: Blackwell Science, 1997.

Ahmad, Ismail Sheikh. *Reading Comprehension Processes and Strategies in L1 and L2 in Malaysian Primary and Secondary Schools* (unpublished doctoral thesis), University of Nottingham, England, 1997.

Koch, Tina. "Establishing Rigour in Qualitative Research: The Decision Trail". *Journal of Advanced Nursing* 53 no. 1 (10 Jan 2006): 91–103, DOI: 10.1111/j.1365-2648.2006.03681.x.

Ledgerwood, Joanna and Victoria White. "Transforming Microfinance Institutions: Providing Full Financial Service to the Poor". Washington, DC: World Bank. DOI: 10.1596/978-0-8213-6615-8, 2006.

Lincoln, Yvonna and Egon Guba. *Naturalistic Inquiry*. Newbury Park, CA: Sage Publications, 1985.

Malterud, Kirsti. "Qualitative Research: Standards, Challenges, and Guidelines". *Lancet* 358 no. 9280 (11 Aug 2001): 483–8.

Marshall, Catherine and Gretchen Rossman. *Designing Qualitative Research*, 2nd ed. Thousand Oaks, California: Sage Publications, 1995.

McCaslin, Mark and Karen Scott. "The Five-Question Method for Framing a Qualitative Research Study". *The Qualitative Report* 8 no. 3 (September 2003): 447–61.

McCosker, Heather, Alan Barnard, and Rod Gerber. "Undertaking Sensitive Research: Issues and Strategies for Meeting the Safety Needs of All Participants". *Forum: Qualitative Social Research* 2, no. 1 (2001): DOI: http://dx.doi.org/10.17169/fqs-2.1.983. Retrieved from http://www.qualitative-research.net/index.php/fqs/article/view/983.

Miles, Matthew and Michael Huberman. *Qualitative Data Analysis: An Expanded Sourcebook*, 2nd ed. Thousand Oaks, CA: Sage Publications, 1994.

Poland, Blake. "Transcription Quality as an Aspect of Rigor in Qualitative Research". *Qualitative Inquiry* 1, no. 3 (1 Sept 1995): 290–310.

Robson, Colin. *Real World Research. A Resource For Social Scientists And Practitioner-Researchers*. Oxford: Blackwell, 1993.

Roller, Margaret and Paul Lavrakas. *Applied Qualitative Research Design: A Total Quality Framework Approach*. New York: Guilford Press, 2015.

Rosnani, Kassim. *Understanding Repeaters in an ESL Writing Course: A Case Study among Pre-Sessional Students* (unpublished doctoral thesis), International Islamic University, Malaysia, 2016.

Sandelowski, Margarete. "The Problem of Rigour in Qualitative Research". *ANS Adv Nurs Sci* 8, no. 3 (Apr 1986): 27–37.

_____ (1998). "Writing a Good Read: Strategies for Re-Presenting Qualitative Data". *Research in Nursing and Health* 21, no. 4 (August 1998): 375–82, DOI: 10.1002/(SICI)1098-240X(199808)21:4<375::AID-NUR9>3.0.CO;2-C.

_____. "Using Qualitative Research". *Qualitative Health Research* 14, no. 10 (2004): 1366–86. DOI: 10.1177/1049732304269672.

Seale, Clive. "Grounding Theory" (87–105). In Seale, C., ed., *The Quality of Qualitative Research*, London: SAGE Publications, 1999.

Sieber, Joan. *Planning Ethically Responsible Research: A Guide for Students and Internal Review Boards.* Newbury Park: SAGE Publications, 1992.

Silverman, David. *Interpreting Qualitative Data: Methods for Analysing Talk, Text and Interaction,* 3rd ed. London: SAGE Publications, 2006.

Strauss, Anselm and Barney Corbin. "Grounded Theory Methodology: An Overview", 173–285. In *The Handbook of Qualitative Research,* Denzin, Norman and Yvonna Lincoln, eds. Thousand Oaks, CA: SAGE Publications, 1994.

Tolich Martin. "Internal Confidentiality: When Confidentiality Assurances Fail Relational Informants". *Qualitative Sociology* 27, no. 1 (March 2004): 101–6.

Yin, Robert. *Case Study Research: Design and Methods,* 4th ed. Thousand Oaks, California: SAGE Publications, 2014.

Printed in the United States
By Bookmasters